DISABILITY STUDIES

AUTISM SPECTRUM DISORDER

AWARENESS AMONG YOUNG ADULTS

Disability Studies

Joav Merrick - Series Editor -

Medical Director, Ministry of Social Affairs,
Jerusalem, Israel

Autism Spectrum Disorder: Awareness among Young Adults
Ronald Chow, Jaclyn Viehweger, Joav Merrick (Editors)
2017. ISBN: 978-1-53612-730-0 (Hardcover)
2017. ISBN: 978-1-53612-731-7 (e-book)

Parkinson's Disease: Awareness among Young Adults
Ronald Chow, Jaclyn Viehweger, Michael Borean, Drew Hollenberg, and Joav Merrick (Editors)
2017. ISBN: 978-1-53612-745-4 (Hardcover)
2017. ISBN: 978-1-53612-746-1 (e-book)

Virtual Reality: Recent Advances in Virtual Rehabilitation System Design
Wendy Powell, Albert "Skip" Rizzo, Paul M. Sharkey and Joav Merrick
2017. ISBN: 978-1-53612-040-0 (Softcover)
2017. ISBN: 978-1-53612-061-5 (e-book)

Child Abuse: Children with Disabilities
Vincent J Palusci, Dena Nazer, Donald E Greydanus and Joav Merrick
2017. ISBN: 978-1-53612-035-6 (Hardcover)
2017. ISBN: 978-1-53612-056-1 (e-book)

Rehabilitation: Innovations and Challenges in the Use of Virtual Reality Technologies
Wendy Powell, Albert "Skip" Rizzo, Paul M. Sharkey and Joav Merrick, (Editors)
2017. ISBN: 978-1-53612-080-6 (Hardcover)
2017. ISBN: 978-1-53612-099-8 (e-book)

Pediatric Pain: Current Aspects
Hatim A. Omar, Dilip R. Patel, Donald E. Greydanus, and Joav Merrick (Editors)
2016. ISBN: 978-1-63485-505-1 (Hardcover)
2016. ISBN: 978-1-63485-537-2 (e-book)

Recent Advances on Using Virtual Reality Technologies for Rehabilitation
Paul M. Sharkey and Joav Merrick (Editors)
2016. ISBN: 978-1-63484-027-9 (Hardcover)
2015. ISBN: 978-1-63484-028-6 (e-book)

Technology, Rehabilitation and Empowerment of People with Special Needs
Lena Pareto, Paul M Sharkey and Joav Merrick (Editors)
2015. ISBN: 978-1-63482-713-3 (Hardcover)
2015. ISBN: 978-1-63482-737-9 (e-book)

Virtual Reality: Rehabilitation in Motor, Cognitive and Sensorial Disorders
Paul M. Sharkey and Joav Merrick (Editors)
2014. ISBN: 978-1-63321-773-7 (Hardcover)
2014. ISBN: 978-1-63321-787-4 (e-book)

Virtual Reality: People with Special Needs
Paul M. Sharkey and Joav Merrick (Editors)
2014. ISBN: 978-1-63321-729-4 (Hardcover)
2014. ISBN: 978-1-63321-734-8 (e-book)

Quality of Life and Intellectual Disability: Knowledge Application to other Social and Educational Challenges
Roy I. Brown and Rhonda M. Faragher (Editors)
2014. ISBN: 978-1-62948-264-4 (Hardcover)
2014. ISBN: 978-1-62948-272-9 (e-book)

Intellectual Disability: Some Current Issues
Joav Merrick, Donald E Greydanus and Dilip R. Patel (Editors)
2014. ISBN: 978-1-63321-855-0 (Hardcover)
2014. ISBN: 978-1-63321-867-3 (e-book)

From One Century to the Next: A History of Wrentham State School and the Institutional Model in Massachusetts
Ingrid Grenon
2014. ISBN: 978-1-63117-711-8 (Hardcover)
2014. ISBN: 978-1-63483-805-4 (Softcover)
2014. ISBN: 978-1-63117-712-5 (e-book)

Pain and the Elderly
Joav Merrick and Mimi M.Y. Tse
2013. ISBN: 978-1-62948-468-6 (Hardcover)
2013. ISBN: 978-1-62948-475-4 (e-book)

Pain: International Research in Pain Management
Joav Merrick, Patricia Schofield and Mohammed Morad (Editors)
2013. ISBN: 978-1-62948-423-5 (Hardcover)
2013. ISBN: 978-1-62948-435-8 (e-book)

Disability and Chronic Disease
Joav Merrick, Shoshana Aspler and Mohammed Morad (Editors)
2013. ISBN: 978-1-62948-288-0 (Hardcover)
2013. ISBN: 978-1-62948-307-8 (e-book)

Down Syndrome and Dementia. A Comprehensive and Historical Review
Vee P. Prasher
2012. ISBN: 978-1-62081-263-1 (Hardcover)
2012. ISBN: 978-1-62081-271-6 (e-book)

Rett Syndrome: Therapeutic Interventions
Meir Lotan and Joav Merrick (Editors)
2011. ISBN: 978-1-61728-614-8 (Hardcover)
2011. ISBN: 978-1-61728-080-1 (Softcover)
2011. ISBN: 978-1-61761-131-5 (e-book)

Pain Management Yearbook 2010
Joav Merrick (Editor)
2011. ISBN: 978-1-61209-972-9 (Hardcover)
2011. ISBN: 978-1-62808-255-5 (e-book)

Pain Management Yearbook 2009
Joav Merrick (Editor)
2011. ISBN: 978-1-61209-666-7 (Hardcover)
2011. ISBN: 978-1-62081-774-2 (e-book)

Pain. Brain Stimulation in the Treatment of Pain
Helena Knotkova, Ricardo Cruciani and Joav Merrick (Editors)
2011. ISBN: 978-1-60876-690-1 (Hardcover)
2011. ISBN: 978-1-61470-495-9 (e-book)

Neural Plasticity in Chronic Pain
Helena Knotkova, Ricardo A. Cruciani and Joav Merrick (Editors)
2011. ISBN: 978-1-61324-657-3 (Hardcover)
2011. ISBN: 978-1-62417-407-0 (e-book)

Disability from a Humanistic Perspective: Towards a Better Quality of Life
Shunit Reiter
2011. ISBN: 978-1-60456-412-9 (Hardcover)
2011. ISBN: 978-1-63117-654-8 (e-book)

Cancer in Children and Adults with Intellectual Disabilities: Current Research Aspects
Daniel Satgé and Joav Merrick (Editors)
2011. ISBN: 978-1-61761-856-7 (Hardcover)
2011. ISBN: 978-1-61122-187-9 (e-book)

Contemporary Issues in Intellectual Disabilities
V. P. Prasher
2010. ISBN: 978-1-61668-023-7 (Hardcover)
2010. ISBN: 978-1-61209-292-8 (e-book)

Virtual Reality: Recent Advances for Health and Wellbeing
Wendy Powell, Paul M Sharkey and Albert "Skip" Rizzo
2017. ISBN: 978-1-53612-454-5 (Softcover)
2017. ISBN: 978-1-53612-455-2 (e-book)

DISABILITY STUDIES

AUTISM SPECTRUM DISORDER

AWARENESS AMONG YOUNG ADULTS

RONALD CHOW
JACLYN VIEHWEGER
AND
JOAV MERRICK
EDITORS

nova
biomedical
New York

Library of Congress Cataloging-in-Publication Data

ISBN: 978-1-53612-730-0

Published by Nova Science Publishers, Inc. † New York

CONTENTS

INTRODUCTION

In: Autism Spectrum Disorder ISBN: 978-1-53612-730-0
Editors: R. Chow, J. Viehweger et al. ©2017 Nova Science Publishers, Inc.

Chapter 1

ARE YOUNG ADULTS AWARE OF AUTISM SPECTRUM DISORDER?

Ronald Chow*[1,*]*, BMSc(C), Jaclyn Viehweger*[1]*, BMSc(C) and Joav Merrick*[2-6]*, MD, MMedSc, DMSc

[1]Infinitas Research Group, London, Ontario, Canada,
[2]National Institute of Child Health and Human Development, Jerusalem, Israel,
[3]Office of the Medical Director, Health Services, Division for Intellectual and Developmental Disabilities, Ministry of Social Affairs and Social Services, Jerusalem, Israel,
[4]Division of Pediatrics, Hadassah Hebrew University Medical Centre, Mt Scopus Campus, Jerusalem, Israel,
[5]Kentucky Children's Hospital, University of Kentucky College of Medicine, Lexington, Kentucky, US and
[6]Center for Healthy Development, School of Public Health, Georgia State University, Atlanta, US

[*] Correspondence: Ronald Chow BMSc(C), Infinitas Research Group, London, Ontario, Canada. Email: rchow48@uwo.ca.

People with autism spectrum disorder (ASD) display deficits/unusual behavior in one of the three domains: Reciprocal social interaction, communication and restricted/repetitive interests/behaviours. The cause of ASD is still unknown, with etiological theories continuing to change as research progresses. It was once proposed that child-rearing was a major determinant, but more recent studies have suggested that the cause is multi-factorial, with genetics playing a substantial part in etiology. Since awareness seems to be a precursor of increased prevalence, it would be interesting to note the awareness amongst young adults, who are the future parents of the society. The awareness of these individuals may allow for extrapolation to predict whether future prevalence of ASD will increase or decrease. In this book we describe the awareness of young adults from Canada, United States, United Kingdom and Asia with respect to ASD.

INTRODUCTION

Autism spectrum disorder (ASD) is a range of neurodevelopmental disorders described in 2013 in the diagnostic and statistical manual of mental disorders (DSM-5) by the American Psychiatric Association (1). This new manual redefined the autism spectrum disorders to encompass the previous (DSM-IV-TR) diagnoses of autism, Asperger syndrome, pervasive developmental disorder not otherwise specified (PDD-NOS) and childhood disintegrative disorder (1). People with ASD display deficits/unusual behavior in one of the three domains: reciprocal social interaction, communication and restricted/repetitive interests/behaviours. Disorders in the social interaction setting manifest themselves in the lack of social-emotional reciprocity, failure to seek to share employment, and poor use of nonverbal communications; communication disorders include difficulties in acquiring speech without compensating through alternative communication methods, use of stereotyped speech and delayed echolalia (1).

The cause of ASD is still unknown, with etiological theories continuing to change as research progresses. It was once proposed that child-rearing was a major determinant, but more recent studies have suggested that the cause is multi-factorial, with genetics playing a substantial part in etiology (2). There also exist rare cases of ASD, where the disorder is developed secondary to other morbidities, such as tuberous sclerosis, fragile X syndrome, phenylketonuria and rubella (2-7).

The prevalence of the disorder has increased over the past several decades, and now noticed in 14.6 per 1,000 (one in 68) children aged 8 years (8-12). The increased prevalence may be a result of greater public awareness of ASD, broadening of diagnostic concepts, reclassification of disease and improved detection (13, 14). ASD is also more likely to affect males than females with estimated prevalence significantly higher among boys aged 8 years (23.6 per 1,000) than among girls aged 8 years (5.3 per 1,000) (12).

Since awareness seems to be a precursor of increased prevalence, it would be interesting to note the awareness amongst young adults, who are the future parents of the society. The awareness of these individuals may allow for extrapolation to predict whether future prevalence of ASD will increase or decrease. The enclosed collection of works details the awareness of young adults with respect to ASD.

ACKNOWLEDGMENTS

We would like to thank Michael Borean and Drew Hollenberg for their support.

REFERENCES

[1] American Psychiatric Association. Diagnostic and statistical manual of mental disorders (DSM-5). Arlington, VA: American Psychiatric Association, 2013.

[2] Bailey A, Le Couteur A, Gottesman I, Bolton P, Simonoff E, Yuzda E, et al. Autism as a strongly genetic disorder: Evidence from a British twin study. Psychol Med 1995;25:63-77.

[3] Marco EJ, Shuse DH. Autism-lessons from the X-chromosome. Soc Cogn Affect Neurosci 2006;1:183-93.

[4] Kothur K, Ray M, Malhi P. Correlation of autism with temporal tubers in tuberous sclerosis complex. Neurol India 2008;56:74-6.

[5] Muhle R, Trentacoste SV, Rapin I. The genetics of autism. Pediatrics 2004;113(5):e472-86.

[6] Bolton PF, Park RJ, Higgins JN, Griffiths PD, Pickles A. Neuro-epileptic determinants of autism spectrum disorder in tuberous sclerosis complex. Brain 2002;125:1247-55.

[7] Trottier G, Srivastava L, Walker CD. Etiology of infantile autism: a review of recent advances in genetic and neurobiological research. J Psychiatry Neurosci 1999;24:103-15.

[8] Chakrabarti S, Fombonne E. Pervasive developmental disorders in preschool children. JAMA 2001;285:3093-9.

[9] Chakrabarti S, Fombonne E. Pervasive development disorders in preschool children: confirmation of high prevalence. Am J Psychiatry 2005;162:1133-41.

[10] Bertrand J, Mars A, Boyle C, Bove F, Yeargin-Allsop M, DeCoufle P. Prevalence of autism in a United States population: The Brick Township, New Jersey, investigation. Pediatrics 2001;108:1155-61.

[11] Yeargin-Allsop M, Rice C, Karapurkar T, Doernberg N, Boyle C, Murphy C. Prevalence of autism in a US metropolitan area. JAMA 2003;289:49-55.

[12] Christensen DL, Baio J, Van Naarden Braun K, Bilder D, Charles J, Constantino JN, et al. Prevalence and characteristics of autism spectrum disorder among children aged 8 years: Autism and Developmental Disabilities Monitoring Network, 11 Sites, United States, 2012. MMWR Surveill Summ 2016;65(3):1-23. doi: 10.15585/mmwr.ss6503a1.

[13] Fombonne E, Zakarian R, Bennett A, Meng L, McLean-Heywood D. Pervasive developmental disorders in Montreal, Quebec, Canada: Prevalence and links with immunization. Pediatrics 2006;118:e139-50.

[14] Shattuck PT. The combination of diagnostic substitution to the growing administrative prevalence of autism in US special education data. Pediatrics 2006;117:1028-37.

SECTION ONE: CANADA

In: Autism Spectrum Disorder ISBN: 978-1-53612-730-0
Editors: R. Chow, J. Viehweger et al. ©2017 Nova Science Publishers, Inc.

Chapter 2

ASSESSING AWARENESS OF AUTISM SPECTRUM DISORDER: ABOUT THE SURVEY INSTRUMENT

Ronald Chow**, BMSc(C)
and Jaclyn Viehweger, BMSc(C)
Infinitas Research Group, London, Ontario, Canada

The aim of our survey was to assess the perceived and actual awareness level of young adults on the topic of autism spectrum disorder. The survey was three pages, and was circulated via media outlets (i.e., email, social media). The first page was a consent form detailing why the study was done, the benefits/costs and other important information regarding the consent process. The second page collected demographic information of respondents. The third page assessed the perceived and actual knowledge of participants. The first question assessed participant's perceived knowledge, and was an agree-neutral-disagree response to the statement that the participant was knowledgeable about Parkinson's disease. The subsequent eight questions were true-false questions to note the knowledge of participants.

* Correspondence: Ronald Chow BMSc(C), Infinitas Research Group, London, Ontario, Canada. Email: rchow48@uwo.ca.

INTRODUCTION

Autism spectrum disorder (ASD) has been reported to be increasing in prevalence, and a driver of that may be a greater public awareness of the disease (1-2). The aim of our survey was to assess the awareness of young adults, who are the future parents of the society and hence a major determinant of the prevalence of the disorder (3).

QUESTIONNAIRE

A three-page questionnaire was designed using Google Forms (see Figures 1-3), and circulated to young adults via media outlets (i.e., email, social media). The questionnaire was voluntary and typically circulated using the following promotional statement:

> Autism is the fastest growing and most commonly diagnosed neurological disorder in Canada. The prevalence of autism has increased over 100% in the last 10 years. This is a startling rate for a disease not many may know much about. Infinitas Research Group has decided to assess the awareness of this disease across the globe.
>
> Please help us out and make this world a better place, by taking a few minutes to quickly fill out this survey: https://docs.google.com/forms/d/e/1FAIpQLSdP-oV_dhKy5LzjElPw3SYzAfGPZXhoP0jEtHxzgVJF6xeHhA/viewform

The first page was a consent form detailing the reason the study is being undertaken, the benefits/costs and also a query requiring participants to consent to the study to progress to the subsequent pages (see Figure 1). For respondents who did not consent to the study, they were thanked for their time and did not progress to the next page.

The second page contained five questions to collect demographic information. The first question asked participants to report their primary location of residence - for young adults who attended postsecondary institutions outside of their home municipality, they were requested to note their institution's district as their region of residence. Participants were also asked to note the age group they belong to - under 18 years old, 18-19 years old, 20-22 years old and over 22 years old. Respondents were given the option not to confide about their sex. The final two questions of the page inquired about whether individuals know of a family member affected by ASD, and whether they know of a friend who is affected by ASD (see Figure 2).

Awareness of Autism Spectrum Disorder

INFORMED CONSENT TO PARTICIPATE IN A RESEARCH STUDY

Principal Investigator: Ronald Chow
Infinitas Research Group
London, ON, Canada
infinitasresearchgroup@gmail.com
https://sites.google.com/view/infinitasresearchgroup/about-us

Co Investigators: Jaclyn Viehweger, Tharani Anpalagan

INFORMED CONSENT

You are being asked to consider participating in a research study. A research study is a way of gathering information on something that is not well understood.

Participating in this study is your choice (voluntary). You have the right to choose not to participate, or to stop participating in this study at any time.

INTRODUCTION

You are being asked to consider participating in this study because you are a young adult.

WHY IS THE STUDY BEING DONE?

Autism spectrum disorder is being ever-more prevalent in the today's society. The purpose of this study is to investigate the current awareness and knowledge surrounding autism among young adults.

Figure 1. Survey (page 1).

BENEFITS AND COSTS

There are no direct benefits or costs to participating in the study. The results from this survey may be published in a manuscript, and benefit the scientific community.

HOW WILL MY INFORMATION BE SECURE?

The study is anonymous, and therefore no names or personal information with be involved in the process.

WHAT ARE THE RIGHTS OF PARTICIPANTS IN A RESEARCH STUDY?

You have the right to receive all information that could help you make a decision about participating in this study. You also have the right to ask questions about this study and your rights as a research participant, and to have them answered to your satisfaction, before you make any decision. You also have the right to ask questions and to receive answers throughout this study.

If you have any questions about this study you may contact the person in charge of this study, the Principal Investigator.

DOCUMENTATION OF INFORMED CONSENT

Participant
By consenting to this form, I confirm that:

- This research study has been fully explained to me and all of my questions answered to my satisfaction
- I understand the requirements of participating in this research study
- I have been informed of the risks and benefits, if any, of participating in this research study
- I have been informed of any alternatives to participating in this research study
- I have been informed of the rights of research participants
- I have this form in its entirety
- I have agreed, or agree to allow the person I am responsible for, to participate in this research study

* Required

Notice of Consent *

○ "Yes, I consent to this form"

○ "No, I do not consent to this form"

NEXT

Figure 1. Survey (page 1 continued).

Awareness of Autism Spectrum Disorder

Demographics of Respondents

Which city do you live in for the majority of the year? *

If you are a post-secondary student, where is your institution located?

- ○ Boone, USA
- ○ Dublin, IRELAND
- ○ Halifax, CANADA
- ○ Hamilton, CANADA
- ○ Ithaca, USA
- ○ Kingston, CANADA
- ○ London, CANADA
- ○ Montreal, CANADA
- ○ New York City, USA
- ○ Rochester, USA
- ○ Saskatoon, CANADA
- ○ Singapore, SINGAPORE
- ○ Toronto, CANADA
- ○ Waterloo, CANADA
- ○ Other: ______

What age group do you belong to? *

- ○ Under 18 years old
- ○ 18-19 years old
- ○ 20-22 years old
- ○ Older than 22 years old

What is your sex? *

- ○ Female
- ○ Male
- ○ Prefer not to say

Figure 2. Survey (page 2).

To your knowledge, do you have a family member affected by autism spectrum disorder? *

- ○ Yes
- ○ No

To your knowledge, do you have a friend affected by autism spectrum disorder?

- ○ Yes
- ○ No

BACK NEXT

Figure 2. Survey (page 2 continued).

Awareness of Autism Spectrum Disorder

Assessment of Knowledge

Please answer these questions as honestly as possible without aid of any kind

I believe I am knowledgeable about Autism

- ○ Agree
- ○ Neutral
- ○ Disagree

Autism is a life-long developmental condition

- ○ True
- ○ False
- ○ Not Sure

Figure 3. Survey (page 3).

Autism can be caused by poor parenting or parental behaviour

○ True

○ False

○ Not Sure

The prevalence of autism has increased over the years

○ True

○ False

○ Not Sure

Autism can arise from vaccinations

○ True

○ False

○ Not Sure

Individuals with autism always prefer to be alone

○ True

○ False

○ Not Sure

People with autism are eccentric geniuses

○ True

○ False

○ Not Sure

Individuals with autism can grow out of it

○ True

○ False

○ Not Sure

Figure 3. Survey (page 3 continued).

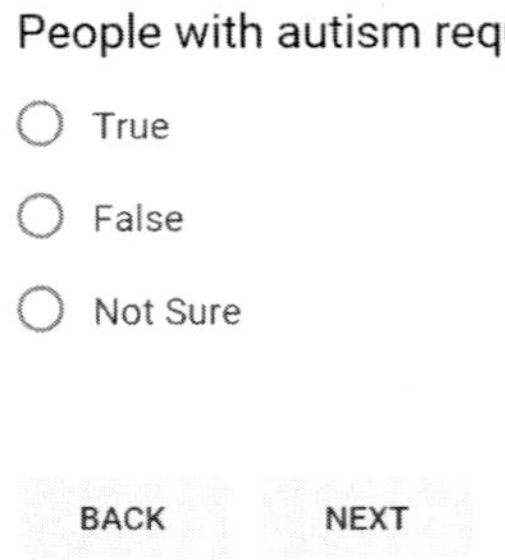
People with autism require substantial medical assistance

True

False

Not Sure

BACK NEXT

Figure 3. Survey (page 3 continued).

The third and final page was designed to evaluate the perceived and actual awareness of ASD. The first question asked participants to respond either agree, neutral or disagree with the statement that the participant was knowledgeable about autism spectrum disorder. All subsequent assessment questions were multiple-choice questions, with the responses of “true,” “false” and “not sure.” The correct answers of the questions are as follows:

1. “Autism is a life-long developmental disorder” - TRUE
2. “Autism can be caused by poor parenting or parental behaviour” - FALSE
3. “The prevalence of autism has increased over the years” - TRUE
4. “Autism can arise from vaccinations” - FALSE
5. “Individuals with autism always prefer to be alone” - FALSE
6. “People with autism are eccentric geniuses” - FALSE
7. “Individuals with autism can grow out of it” - FALSE
8. “People with autism require substantial medical assistance” - FALSE

Statistical analysis

Descriptive statistics were used to portray the participant demographics. For each participant, the number of correct answers was noted. The number of people who answered a question correctly was also recorded.

Respondents who had four or less correct responses were deemed not knowledgeable; 5-6 correct responses led to the respondent classified as having satisfactory knowledge, and a score in excess of seven was viewed as knowledgeable.

Fisher exact tests were used to compared the percentage of subgroups (age, gender, familial ties) who answered correctly/incorrectly, and ANOVA procedures (using pooled means) were used to compare the average scores between the subgroups. P-values less than 0.05 were considered statistically significant. All statistical analyses were conducted using the Statistical Analysis Software (SAS Version 9.4 for Windows).

ACKNOWLEDGMENTS

We would like to thank Michael Borean, Drew Hollenberg and Tharani Anpalagan for their support/assistance in the development of the questionnaire.

REFERENCES

[1] Fombonne E, Zakarian R, Bennett A, Meng L, McLean-Heywood D. Pervasive developmental disorders in Montreal, Quebec, Canada: Prevalence and links with immunization. Pediatrics 2006;118:e139-50.

[2] Shattuck PT. The combination of diagnostic substitution to the growing administrative prevalence of autism in US special education data. Pediatrics 2006;117:1028-37.

[3] Chow R, Viehweger J. Are young adults aware of autism spectrum disorder? Int Public Health J 2019;11(1), in press.

In: Autism Spectrum Disorder ISBN: 978-1-53612-730-0
Editors: R. Chow, J. Viehweger et al. ©2017 Nova Science Publishers, Inc.

Chapter 3

AWARENESS OF AUTISM SPECTRUM DISORDER AMONG YOUNG ADULTS IN LONDON, CANADA

Ronald Chow*[1,*], *BMSc(C), Jaclyn Viehweger*[1], *BMSc(C), Tharani Anpalagan*[1], *BMSc(C), Hunster Yang*[2], *BSc(C) and Rishav Banerjee*[2], *BA(C)

[1]Infinitas Research Group, London, Ontario, Canada
[2]Autism Awareness Western, London, Ontario, Canada

Autism spectrum disorder (ASD) has increased in prevalence over the past several decades, with some studies reporting a 15-fold increase. The increased prevalence has been suggested not to be a result of an increase in comorbidities and environmental determinants, but rather a byproduct of heightened awareness of ASD among new parents. Thus, assessing the awareness of current young adults (and the next generation of parents) may provide some insight into whether the prevalence of diagnosed ASD will increase or decrease. A three-page survey was designed and circulated to young adults in London, Ontario, Canada. A total of 50 young adults consented and completed the survey. The awareness level

* Correspondence: Ronald Chow BMSc(C), Infinitas Research Group, London, Ontario, Canada. Email: rchow48@uwo.ca.

(56%) was similar to the perceived awareness (54%). The awareness level was also greater than the proportion of respondents who know of a family member or friend affected by the disorder. Such findings indicate that exposure alone does not lead to awareness of autism, but seems to be a significant determinant.

INTRODUCTION

Autism spectrum disorder (ASD) has increased in prevalence over the past several decades, with some studies reporting a 15-fold increase (1-4). The cause of ASD used to be thought of as a result of poor child-rearing, which was an incorrect theory; more recent postulates suggest that genetics plays a substantial role (5). ASD can also be caused as a result of comorbidities - tuberous sclerosis, fragile X syndrome, and rubella (5-10).

The greater prevalence of diagnosed ASD has been suggested not to be a result of increased prevalence of comorbidities and environmental determinants, but rather a byproduct of heightened awareness of ASD among new parents (11-12). Thus, assessing the awareness of current young adults (and the next generation of parents) may provide some insight into whether the prevalence of diagnosed ASD will increase or decrease (13).

OUR STUDY

A three-page survey was designed and circulated to young adults in London, Ontario, Canada. The first page had a consent form listing the benefits/costs, and required participants to consent in order to complete the questionnaire. The second page collected participant demographics, and the third page assessed the perceived knowledge of ASD and also contained eight assessment questions (14).

Descriptive statistics were used to convey participant demographics, and also the responses provided by respondents. Fisher exact tests were run to investigate whether different subgroups provided different responses.

Subgroup analyses were conducted by age group (under/over 20 years old), sex (males/females), whether they have a family member with ASD, and whether they have a friend with ASD. P-values less than 0.05 were considered statistically significant. All statistical procedures were conducted using the Statistical Analysis Software (SAS Version 9.4 for Windows) (14).

FINDINGS

A total of 50 young adults consented and completed the survey. 40% were between 18 and 19 years old, 40% were between 20 and 22 years old, 16% over 22 years old, and 4% under 18 years old. 4% did not identify their sex; 26% were male and 70% were female. 26% know of a family member affected by ASD, and 44% have one or multiple friends affected by ASD (see Table 1).

Table 1. Demographics

Demographic	**n = 50**
Age Group	
Under 18 years old	2 (4%)
18-19 years old	20 (40%)
20-22 years old	20 (40%)
Over 22 years old	8 (16%)
Sex	
Male	13 (26%)
Female	35 (70%)
Prefer not to say	2 (4%)
Family member affected by Autism Spectrum Disorder	
Yes	13 (26%)
No	37 (74%)
Friend(s) affected by Autism Spectrum Disorder	
Yes	22 (44%)
No	28 (56%)

Table 2. Perceived and actual knowledge

Question Item	n = 50
"I believe I am knowledgeable about Autism"	
Agree	28 (56%)
Disagree	6 (12%)
Neutral	16 (32%)
"Autism is a life-long developmental condition"	
True	47 (94%)
False	0 (0%)
Not Sure	3 (6%)
"Autism can be caused by poor parenting or parental behavior"	
True	0 (0%)
False	46 (92%)
Not Sure	4 (8%)
"The prevalence of Autism has increased over the years"	
True	26 (52%)
False	8 (16%)
Not Sure	16 (32%)
"Autism can arise from vaccinations"	
True	1 (2%)
False	42 (84%)
Not Sure	7 (14%)
"Individuals with Autism always prefer to be alone"	
True	2 (4%)
False	44 (88%)
Not Sure	4 (8%)
"People with Autism are eccentric geniuses"	
True	6 (12%)
False	37 (74%)
Not Sure	7 (14%)
"Individuals with Autism can grow out of it"	
True	2 (4%)
False	39 (78%)
Not Sure	9 (18%)
"People with Autism require substantial medical assistance"	
True	7 (14%)
False	26 (52%)
Not Sure	17 (34%)
Knowledge Score	
Not Knowledgeable (0-4)	7 (14%)
Satisfactory (5-6)	16 (32%)
Knowledgeable (7-8)	27 (54%)

56% considered themselves knowledgeable about autism. 94% remarked that it is a lifelong developmental condition, 92% noted it is not a result of poor parenting, and 52% indicated that the prevalence has increased over the years. 84%, 88% and 74% properly dismissed the statements that autism can arise from vaccination, individuals with autism always prefer to be alone, and that autistic individuals are eccentric geniuses. 78% noted that affected individuals do not grow out of ASD, and 52% noted that individuals do not necessarily require substantial medical assistance. Overall, 54% of respondents were knowledgeable about ASD (7 or 8 out of 8) (see Table 2).

A greater proportion of older individuals remarked they were knowledgeable about ASD (p=0.0202) - 71% vs 36% for those over 20 years old and under 20 years old, respectively. There was no actual difference in knowledge, with 50% and 57% of the two cohorts knowledgeable (p=0.7921). 91% and 96% noted that ASD is a life-long developmental condition (p=0.5727); 100% and 86% indicated that it is not caused by poor parenting (p=0.1207); 50% and 54% answered that the prevalence has increased over the years (p=0.8606); 86% and 82% concluded that it cannot arise from vaccinations (p=0.4233); 86% and 89% remarked that ASD patients do not always prefer to be alone (p=0.9999); 64% and 82% acknowledged that not all individuals are eccentric geniuses (p=0.3358); 82% and 75% answered that individuals cannot grow out of it (p=0.8551); 45% and 57% responded that not all ASD individuals require substantial medical assistance (p=0.7370) (see Table 3).

Females perceived themselves to be more knowledgeable than males (66% vs 31%; p=0.0230), and females were truly more knowledgeable as well (66% vs 23%; p=0.0172). 77% and 100% answered in the affirmative to the statement that it is a lifelong developmental condition (p=0.0165), and 31% and 63% to the statement that the prevalence has increased over the years (p=0.124). 92% and 91% correctly identified that the statement with respect to poor parenting was false (p=0.9999), while 85% and 83% similarly remarked about vaccinations (p=0.9999), 77% and 91% about the statement that ASD individuals prefer to be alone (p=0.2132), 77% and 71% on the statement that ASD individuals are eccentric geniuses (p=0.9999), 62% and 86% about the myth that individuals can grow out of it (p=0.1851), and 15% and 66% that these patients require substantial medical assistance (p=0.554) (see Table 3).

Table 3. Perceived and actual knowledge - by subgroups

Question Item	Under 20 n = 22	Over 20 n = 28	p-value
"I believe I am knowledgeable about Autism"			0.0202
Agree	8 (36%)	20 (71%)	
Disagree	5 (23%)	1 (4%)	
Neutral	9 (41%)	7 (25%)	
"Autism is a life-long developmental condition"			0.5757
True	20 (91%)	27 (96%)	
False	0 (0%)	0 (0%)	
Not Sure	2 (9%)	1 (4%)	
"Autism can be caused by poor parenting or parental behavior"			0.1207
True	0 (0%)	0 (0%)	
False	22 (100%)	24 (86%)	
Not Sure	0 (0%)	4 (14%)	
"The prevalence of Autism has increased over the years"			0.8606
True	11 (50%)	15 (54%)	
False	3 (14%)	5 (18%)	
Not Sure	8 (36%)	8 (29%)	
"Autism can arise from vaccinations"			0.4233
True	1 (5%)	0 (0%)	
False	19 (86%)	23 (82%)	
Not Sure	2 (9%)	5 (18%)	
"Individuals with Autism always prefer to be alone"			0.9999
True	1 (5%)	1 (4%)	
False	19 (86%)	25 (89%)	
Not Sure	2 (9%)	2 (7%)	
"People with Autism are eccentric geniuses"			0.3358
True	4 (18%)	2 (7%)	
False	14 (64%)	23 (82%)	
Not Sure	4 (18%)	3 (11%)	

Question Item	Under 20 n = 22	Over 20 n = 28	p-value
"Individuals with Autism can grow out of it"			0.8551
True	1 (5%)	1 (4%)	
False	18 (82%)	21 (75%)	
Not Sure	3 (14%)	6 (21%)	
"People with Autism require substantial medical assistance"			0.7370
True	3 (14%)	4 (14%)	
False	10 (45%)	16 (57%)	
Not Sure	9 (41%)	8 (29%)	
Knowledge Score			0.7921
Not Knowledgeable (0-4)	4 (18%)	3 (11%)	
Satisfactory (5-6)	7 (32%)	9 (32%)	
Knowledgeable (7-8)	11 (50%)	16 (57%)	
Question Item	**Males n = 13**	**Females n = 35**	
"I believe I am knowledgeable about Autism"			0.0230
Agree	4 (31%)	23 (66%)	
Disagree	1 (7%)	5 (14%)	
Neutral	8 (62%)	7 (20%)	
"Autism is a life-long developmental condition"			0.0165
True	10 (77%)	35 (100%)	
False	0 (0%)	0 (0%)	
Not Sure	3 (23%)	0 (0%)	
"Autism can be caused by poor parenting or parental behavior"			0.9999
True	0 (0%)	0 (0%)	
False	12 (92%)	32 (91%)	
Not Sure	1 (7%)	3 (9%)	
"The prevalence of Autism has increased over the years"			0.1244
True	4 (31%)	22 (63%)	
False	3 (23%)	4 (11%)	
Not Sure	6 (46%)	9 (26%)	
"Autism can arise from vaccinations"			0.9999
True	0 (0%)	1 (3%)	
False	11 (85%)	29 (83%)	
Not Sure	2 (15%)	5 (14%)	

Table 3. (Continued)

Question Item	**Males n = 13**	**Females n = 35**	
"Individuals with Autism always prefer to be alone"			0.2132
True	1 (7%)	1 (3%)	
False	10 (77%)	32 (91%)	
Not Sure	2 (15%)	2 (6%)	
"People with Autism are eccentric geniuses"			0.9999
True	1 (7%)	5 (14%)	
False	10 (77%)	25 (71%)	
Not Sure	2 (15%)	5 (14%)	
"Individuals with Autism can grow out of it"			0.1851
True	1 (7%)	1 (3%)	
False	8 (62%)	30 (86%)	
Not Sure	4 (31%)	4 (11%)	
"People with Autism require substantial medical assistance"			0.0054
True	3 (23%)	4 (11%)	
False	2 (15%)	23 (66%)	
Not Sure	8 (62%)	8 (23%)	
Knowledge Score			0.0172
Not Knowledgeable (0-4)	4 (31%)	3 (9%)	
Satisfactory (5-6)	6 (46%)	9 (26%)	
Knowledgeable (7-8)	3 (23%)	23 (66%)	
Question Item	**Family affected n = 13**	**Family unaffected n = 37**	
"I believe I am knowledgeable about Autism"			0.0103
Agree	12 (92%)	16 (43%)	
Disagree	0 (0%)	6 (16%)	
Neutral	1 (8%)	15 (41%)	
"Autism is a life-long developmental condition"			0.5583
True	13 (100%)	34 (92%)	
False	0 (0%)	0 (0%)	
Not Sure	0 (0%)	3 (8%)	

Question Item	**Family affected n = 13**	**Family unaffected n = 37**	
"Autism can be caused by poor parenting or parental behavior"			0.2746
True	0 (0%)	0 (0%)	
False	11 (85%)	35 (95%)	
Not Sure	2 (15%)	2 (5%)	
"The prevalence of Autism has increased over the years"			0.3361
True	9 (69%)	17 (46%)	
False	2 (15%)	6 (16%)	
Not Sure	2 (15%)	14 (38%)	
"Autism can arise from vaccinations"			0.9999
True	0 (0%)	1 (3%)	
False	11 (85%)	31 (84%)	
Not Sure	2 (15%)	5 (14%)	
"Individuals with Autism always prefer to be alone"			0.9999
True	0 (0%)	2 (5%)	
False	12 (92%)	32 (86%)	
Not Sure	1 (8%)	3 (8%)	
"People with Autism are eccentric geniuses"			0.8763
True	2 (15%)	4 (11%)	
False	9 (69%)	28 (76%)	
Not Sure	2 (15%)	5 (14%)	
"Individuals with Autism can grow out of it"			0.8300
True	0 (0%)	2 (5%)	
False	10 (77%)	29 (78%)	
Not Sure	3 (23%)	6 (16%)	
"People with Autism require substantial medical assistance"			<0.0001
True	7 (54%)	0 (0%)	
False	3 (23%)	23 (62%)	
Not Sure	3 (23%)	14 (38%)	
Knowledge Score			0.9044
Not Knowledgeable (0-4)	1 (8%)	6 (16%)	
Satisfactory (5-6)	4 (31%)	12 (32%)	
Knowledgeable (7-8)	8 (62%)	19 (51%)	

Table 3. (Continued)

Question Item	Friend affected n = 22	Friend unaffected n = 28	
"I believe I am knowledgeable about Autism"			0.2304
Agree	15 (68%)	13 (46%)	
Disagree	1 (5%)	5 (18%)	
Neutral	6 (27%)	10 (36%)	
"Autism is a life-long developmental condition"			0.9999
True	21 (95%)	26 (93%)	
False	0 (0%)	0 (0%)	
Not Sure	1 (5%)	2 (7%)	
"Autism can be caused by poor parenting or parental behavior"			0.1207
True	0 (0%)	0 (0%)	
False	22 (100%)	24 (86%)	
Not Sure	0 (0%)	4 (14%)	
"The prevalence of Autism has increased over the years"			0.3460
True	12 (55%)	14 (50%)	
False	5 (23%)	3 (11%)	
Not Sure	5 (23%)	11 (39%)	
"Autism can arise from vaccinations"			0.0075
True	0 (0%)	1 (4%)	
False	22 (100%)	20 (71%)	
Not Sure	0 (0%)	7 (25%)	
"Individuals with Autism always prefer to be alone"			0.0753
True	0 (0%)	2 (7%)	
False	22 (100%)	22 (79%)	
Not Sure	0 (0%)	4 (14%)	
"People with Autism are eccentric geniuses"			0.0070
True	0 (0%)	6 (21%)	
False	21 (95%)	16 (57%)	
Not Sure	1 (5%)	6 (21%)	
"Individuals with Autism can grow out of it"			0.8551
True	1 (5%)	1 (4%)	
False	18 (82%)	21 (75%)	
Not Sure	3 (14%)	6 (21%)	

Question Item	**Friend affected n = 22**	**Friend unaffected n = 28**	
"People with Autism require substantial medical assistance"			0.2885
True	3 (14%)	4 (14%)	
False	14 (64%)	12 (43%)	
Not Sure	5 (23%)	12 (43%)	
Knowledge Score			0.0115
Not Knowledgeable (0-4)	2 (9%)	5 (18%)	
Satisfactory (5-6)	3 (14%)	13 (46%)	
Knowledgeable (7-8)	17 (77%)	10 (36%)	

Those with family members were not more knowledgeable about the disease than those without an affected member - 62% were knowledgeable, compared to 51% of those unaffected (p=0.9044). Those with an affected family member believed they were more knowledgeable (92% vs 43%; p=0.0103). 100% and 92% answered that it is a lifelong developmental condition (p=0.5583), 85% and 95% noted that it is not caused by poor parenting (p=0.2746), and 69% and 46% concluded that the prevalence has increased over the years (p=0.3361). 85% and 84% noted that it is not a result of vaccinations (p=0.9999), 92% and 86% responded that individuals do not prefer to be alone (p=0.9999), 69% and 76% concluded that ASD individuals are not eccentric geniuses (p=0.8763), 77% and 78% reported that individuals cannot grow out of it (p=0.8300), and 23% and 62% remarked that ASD individuals do not require substantial medical assistance (p<0.0001) (see Table 3).

Those with ASD friends do not perceive themselves to be more knowledgeable than those without friends affected by the disorder - 68% compared to 46% (p=0.2304). 95% and 93% acknowledged that it is a lifelong developmental condition (p=0.9999), 100% and 86% responded that it cannot be caused by parenting (p=0.1207), and 55% and 50% noted that its prevalence has increased over the years (p=0.3460). 100% and 71% concluded that individuals do not prefer to be alone (p=0.0753), 95% and 57% concluded that they are not all eccentric geniuses (p=0.0070), 82% and 75% responded that individuals cannot grow out of it (p=0.8551), and

64% and 43% acknowledged that it does not require substantial medical assistance (p=0.2885). Overall, those with ASD friends were more knowledgeable, with 77% compared to 36% deemed knowledgeable (p=0.0115) (see Table 3).

DISCUSSION

This is the first study to our knowledge to look into the perceived and actual awareness of young adults with respect to ASD. The perceived and actual awareness levels were similar - 56% perceived and 54% actual awareness. These results seem to suggest that those who perceived themselves to be unaware may actually be unaware of ASD. These findings are noticeably different when compared to the awareness of diseases that typically affect the older population (15-20) - that young adults are more aware of the disease than they perceived themselves to be. This improved self-awareness with respect to their knowledge may be a result of greater exposure to ASD compared to Parkinson's (15-17) and Alzheimer's (18-20) disease.

The awareness level (54%) also was in excess of the proportion of respondents who know of a family member (26%) or friend (44%) affected by the disorder. These findings suggest that individuals become aware of ASD outside of mere exposure to the disorder. However, the indication that those with affected friends may be more aware suggests that exposure does play a significant role in terms of knowledgeability about the disorder.

The fact that a greater percentage are aware of ASD compared to the percentage of those with an affected friend may also indicate that the incidence of ASD may continue to rise in the next decades as this population enters parenthood. However, further longitudinal investigations need to be conducted to quantitatively study such a suggestion.

This study was not without limitations. Since this was a survey study, there exists the possibility of a response/sampling bias. However, the sample size should hopefully normalize the data to reduce the effect size of any anomalies.

In conclusion, the awareness level was similar to the perceived awareness. The awareness level was also greater than the proportion of respondents who know of a family member or friend affected by the disorder. Such findings indicate that exposure alone does not lead to awareness of autism, but seems to be a significant determinant.

ACKNOWLEDGMENTS

Rishav Banerjee has ASD. We would like to thank Michael Borean and Drew Hollenberg for their support.

REFERENCES

[1] Chakrabarti S, Fombonne E. Pervasive developmental disorders in preschool children. JAMA 2001;285:3093-9.

[2] Chakrabarti S, Fombonne E. Pervasive development disorders in preschool children: confirmation of high prevalence. Am J Psychiatry 2005;162:1133-41.

[3] Bertrand J, Mars A, Boyle C, Bove F, Yeargin-Allsop M, DeCoufle P. Prevalence of autism in a United States population: The Brick Township, New Jersey, investigation. Pediatrics 2001;108:1155-61.

[4] Yeargin-Allsop M, Rice C, Karapurkar T, Doernberg N, Boyle C, Murphy C. Prevalence of autism in a US metropolitan area. JAMA 2003;289:49-55.

[5] Bailey A, Le Couteur A, Gottesman I, Bolton P, Simonoff E, Yuzda E, et al. Autism as a strongly genetic disorder: evidence from a British twin study. Psychol Med 1995;25:63-77.

[6] Marco EJ, Shuse DH. Autism-lessons from the X-chromosome. Soc Cogn Affect Neurosci 2006;1:183-93.

[7] Kothur K, Ray M, Malhi P. Correlation of autism with temporal tubers in tuberous sclerosis complex. Neurol India 2008;56:74-6.

[8] Muhle R, Trentacoste SV, Rapin I. The genetics of autism. Pediatrics 2004;113:e472-86.

[9] Bolton PF, Park RJ, Higgins JN, Griffiths PD, Pickles A. Neuro-epileptic determinants of autism spectrum disorder in tuberous sclerosis complex. Brain 2002;125:1247-55.

[10] Trottier G, Srivastava L, Walker CD. Etiology of infantile autism: a review of recent advances in genetic and neurobiological research. J Psychiatr Neurosci 1999;24:103-15.

[11] Fombonne E, Zakarian R, Bennett A, Meng L, McLean-Heywood D. Pervasive developmental disorders in Montreal, Quebec, Canada: Prevalence and links with immunization. Pediatrics 2006;118:e139-50.

[12] Shattuck PT. The combination of diagnostic substitution to the growing administrative prevalence of autism in US special education data. Pediatrics 2006;117:1028-37.

[13] Chow R, Viehweger J. Are young adults aware of autism spectrum disorder? Int Public Health J 2019;11(1), in press.

[14] Chow R, Viehweger J. Assessing awareness of autism spectrum disorder: About the survey instrument. Int Public Health J 2019;11(1), in press.

[15] Chow R, Viehweger J, Trasente V, Borean M, Hollenberg D, Lam M, et al. Awareness of Parkinson's disease among young adults in London, Canada. J Pain Manage 2019;12(1), in press.

[16] Ho S, Viehweger J, Trasente V, Ho C, Ng W, Wong M, et al. Awareness of Parkinson's disease among young adults in Toronto, Canada. J Pain Manage 2019;12(1), in press.

[17] Viehweger J, Chow R, Trasente V, Duarte N, Borean M, Hollenberg D, et al. Awareness of Parkinson's disease among young adults in Waterloo, Canada. J Pain Manage 2019;12(1), in press.

[18] Chow R, Ferrara A, Borean M, Hollenberg D, Lam M, Anpalagan T, et al. Awareness of Alzheimer's disease among young adults in London, Canada. Int J Child Health Hum Dev 2018; in press.

[19] Chow R, Borean M, Hollenberg D, Midroni L, Midroni C, Kim Y, et al. Awareness of Alzheimer's disease among young adults in Kingston, Canada. Int J Child Health Hum Dev 2018; in press.

[20] Borean M, Rzepka A, Trasente V, Hollenberg D, Ho C, Ng W, et al. Awareness of Alzheimer's disease among young adults in Toronto, Canada. Int J Child Health Hum Dev 2018; in press.

In: Autism Spectrum Disorder ISBN: 978-1-53612-730-0
Editors: R. Chow, J. Viehweger et al. ©2017 Nova Science Publishers, Inc.

Chapter 4

Awareness of Autism Spectrum Disorder among Young Adults in Toronto, Canada

Ronald Chow*[*], *BMSc(C), Jaclyn Viehweger, BMSc(C), Drew Hollenberg, BMSc(C), Cynthia Ho, BA(C), Wesley Ng, BSc(C) and Matthew Wong, BA AS(C)

Infinitas Research Group, London, Ontario, Canada

The number of individuals diagnosed with autism spectrum disorder (ASD) has increased over the past several decades. It has been suspected that this is a result of parents being more aware of ASD and consequently bringing their children forth for examination and diagnosis. Assessing the awareness of ASD in today's young adults (the next generation of parents) may allow us to catch a glimpse of the future prevalence of the disorder. The aim of this study was to look into the perceived and actual awareness of young adults with respect to ASD in Toronto, Canada. A three-page survey was designed and circulated. 85 individuals completed the survey. 29% were aware of ASD, which is lower than the perceived awareness level of 34%. The awareness level is greater than the

[*] Correspondence: Ronald Chow BMSc(C), Infinitas Research Group, London, Ontario, Canada. Email: rchow48@uwo.ca.

percentage of individuals with family members affected by ASD (26%) but lower than the percentage of individuals with friends affected by ASD (45%). This suggests that exposure to family, and not friends, may contribute a greater role to ASD awareness.

INTRODUCTION

The number of individuals diagnosed with autism spectrum disorder (ASD) has increased over the past several decades (1-4). It has been suspected that this is a result of parents being more aware of ASD and consequently bringing their children forth for examination and diagnosis (5, 6). Assessing the awareness of ASD in today's young adults (the next generation of parents) may allow us to catch a glimpse of the future prevalence of the disorder (7).

A study was conducted in London, Canada, to assess the knowledge of young adults with respect to ASD. The results indicate that 44% have a friend with the disorder, which is lower than the 56% awareness rate. The data suggests that mere exposure is not the only determinant of awareness, and that future prevalence could potentially increase further as a result of great awareness (8). There should also be further studies to look into whether the awareness rate is higher than the percentage of individuals affected by ASD, as other similar studies have indicated that variation exists between geographic locations (9-14). The aim of this study was to look into the perceived and actual awareness of young adults with respect to ASD in Toronto, Canada.

OUR STUDY

A three-page survey was designed and circulated to young adults in Toronto, Ontario, Canada. The first page had a consent form listing the benefits/costs, and required participants to consent in order to complete the questionnaire. The second page collected participant demographics, and the third page assessed the perceived knowledge of ASD and also contained eight assessment questions (15).

Descriptive statistics were used to convey participant demographics, and also the responses provided by respondents. Fisher exact tests were run to investigate whether different subgroups provided different responses. Subgroup analyses were conducted by age group (under/over 20 years old), sex (males/females), whether they have a family member with ASD, and whether they have a friend with ASD. P-values less than 0.05 were considered statistically significant. All statistical procedures were conducted using the Statistical Analysis Software (SAS Version 9.4 for Windows) (15).

WHAT WE FOUND

85 individuals completed the survey, of which 42 (49%) were between 18 and 19 years old, 22 (26%) were between 20 and 22 years old, 12 (14%) were under 18 years old, and 9 (11%) were over 22 years old. Three-quarters (75%) reported as female, 22% noted they were male, and 2% did not identify their sex. 26% had a family member affected by ASD, and 45% knew of a friend affected by ASD (see Table 1).

34% of participants believed they were knowledgeable about ASD. 79% noted that ASD is a lifelong condition, 85% answered that it is not caused by parenting, 66% indicated that its prevalence has increased over the years, and 74% concluded that it can arise from vaccinations. 82% answered that individuals do not always prefer to be alone, 61% responded that they are not all eccentric geniuses, 56% remarked that individuals cannot grow out of it, and 49% noted that people do not require substantial medical assistance. Overall, 29% were knowledgeable about ASD (see Table 2).

Table 1. Demographics

Demographic	n = 85
Age Group	
Under 18 years old	12 (14%)
18-19 years old	42 (49%)
20-22 years old	22 (26%)
Over 22 years old	9 (11%)
Sex	
Male	19 (22%)
Female	64 (75%)
Prefer not to say	2 (2%)
Family member affected by Autism	
Yes	22 (26%)
No	63 (74%)
Friend(s) affected by Autism	
Yes	38 (45%)
No	47 (55%)

There was no difference in perceived and actual awareness between the age groups. 35% of those under 20 years old and 32% of those over 20 years old believed they were aware of ASD (p=0.9446). 78% and 81% of the two groups, respectively, noted that it is a lifelong developmental condition (p=0.8950), 87% and 81% answered it was not caused by poor parenting (p=0.4889), 63% and 71% concluded that it has increased over the years (p=0.7917), 69% and 84% remarked that it was not caused by vaccinations (p=0.3503), and 78% and 90% responded that those with ASD do not prefer to always be alone (p=0.0579). 50% and 81% indicated that ASD individuals are not eccentric geniuses (p=0.0098), 54% and 61% noted that individuals cannot grow out of it (p=0.8769), and 50% and 48% remarked that afflicted individuals do not require substantial medical assistance (p=0.9142). 28% and 32% were deemed knowledgeable (p=0.3021) (see Table 3).

Table 2. Perceived and actual knowledge

Question Item	n = 85
"I believe I am knowledgeable about Autism"	
Agree	29 (34%)
Disagree	8 (9%)
Neutral	48 (56%)
"Autism is a life-long developmental condition"	
True	67 (79%)
False	2 (2%)
Not Sure	16 (19%)
"Autism can be caused by poor parenting or parental behavior"	
True	3 (4%)
False	72 (85%)
Not Sure	10 (12%)
"The prevalence of Autism has increased over the years"	
True	56 (66%)
False	4 (5%)
Not Sure	25 (29%)
"Autism can arise from vaccinations"	
True	4 (5%)
False	63 (74%)
Not Sure	18 (21%)
"Individuals with Autism always prefer to be alone"	
True	7 (8%)
False	70 (82%)
Not Sure	8 (9%)
"People with Autism are eccentric geniuses"	
True	10 (12%)
False	52 (61%)
Not Sure	23 (27%)
"Individuals with Autism can grow out of it"	
True	6 (7%)
False	48 (56%)
Not Sure	31 (36%)
"People with Autism require substantial medical assistance"	
True	18 (21%)
False	42 (49%)
Not Sure	25 (29%)
Knowledge Score	
Not Knowledgeable (0-4)	22 (26%)
Satisfactory (5-6)	38 (45%)
Knowledgeable (7-8)	25 (29%)

Table 3. Perceived and actual knowledge - by subgroups

Question Item	Under 20 n = 54	Over 20 n = 31	p-value
"I believe I am knowledgeable about Autism"			0.9446
Agree	19 (35%)	10 (32%)	
Disagree	5 (9%)	3 (10%)	
Neutral	30 (56%)	18 (58%)	
"Autism is a life-long developmental condition"			0.8950
True	42 (78%)	25 (81%)	
False	1 (2%)	1 (3%)	
Not Sure	11 (20%)	5 (16%)	
"Autism can be caused by poor parenting or parental behavior"			0.4889
True	1 (2%)	2 (6%)	
False	47 (87%)	25 (81%)	
Not Sure	6 (11%)	4 (13%)	
"The prevalence of Autism has increased over the years"			0.7917
True	34 (63%)	22 (71%)	
False	3 (6%)	1 (3%)	
Not Sure	17 (31%)	8 (26%)	
"Autism can arise from vaccinations"			0.3503
True	3 (6%)	1 (3%)	
False	37 (69%)	26 (84%)	
Not Sure	14 (26%)	4 (13%)	
"Individuals with Autism always prefer to be alone"			0.0579
True	4 (7%)	3 (10%)	
False	42 (78%)	28 (90%)	
Not Sure	8 (15%)	0 (0%)	
"People with Autism are eccentric geniuses"			0.0098
True	7 (13%)	3 (10%)	
False	27 (50%)	25 (81%)	
Not Sure	20 (37%)	3 (10%)	
"Individuals with Autism can grow out of it"			0.8769
True	4 (7%)	2 (6%)	
False	29 (54%)	19 (61%)	
Not Sure	21 (39%)	10 (32%)	

Question Item	Under 20 n = 54	Over 20 n = 31	p-value
"People with Autism require substantial medical assistance"			0.9142
True	12 (22%)	6 (19%)	
False	27 (50%)	15 (48%)	
Not Sure	15 (28%)	10 (32%)	
Knowledge Score			0.3021
Not Knowledgeable (0-4)	17 (31%)	5 (16%)	
Satisfactory (5-6)	22 (41%)	16 (52%)	
Knowledgeable (7-8)	15 (28%)	10 (32%)	
Question Item	**Males n = 19**	**Females n = 64**	
"I believe I am knowledgeable about Autism"			0.0868
Agree	10 (53%)	19 (30%)	
Disagree	0 (0%)	8 (13%)	
Neutral	9 (47%)	37 (58%)	
"Autism is a life-long developmental condition"			0.7044
True	17 (89%)	49 (77%)	
False	0 (0%)	2 (3%)	
Not Sure	2 (11%)	13 (20%)	
"Autism can be caused by poor parenting or parental behavior"			0.4119
True	1 (5%)	1 (2%)	
False	17 (89%)	55 (86%)	
Not Sure	1 (5%)	8 (13%)	
"The prevalence of Autism has increased over the years"			0.7347
True	14 (74%)	41 (64%)	
False	1 (5%)	3 (5%)	
Not Sure	4 (21%)	20 (31%)	
"Autism can arise from vaccinations"			0.4150
True	2 (11%)	2 (3%)	
False	14 (74%)	49 (77%)	
Not Sure	3 (16%)	13 (20%)	
"Individuals with Autism always prefer to be alone"			0.5678
True	3 (16%)	4 (6%)	
False	15 (79%)	54 (84%)	
Not Sure	1 (5%)	6 (9%)	

Table 3. (Continued)

Question Item	**Males n = 19**	**Females n = 64**	
"People with Autism are eccentric geniuses"			0.2338
True	2 (11%)	8 (13%)	
False	9 (47%)	42 (66%)	
Not Sure	8 (42%)	14 (22%)	
"Individuals with Autism can grow out of it"			0.8395
True	1 (5%)	5 (8%)	
False	10 (53%)	38 (59%)	
Not Sure	8 (42%)	21 (33%)	
"People with Autism require substantial medical assistance"			0.5790
True	5 (26%)	12 (19%)	
False	10 (53%)	32 (50%)	
Not Sure	4 (21%)	20 (31%)	
Knowledge Score			0.9999
Not Knowledgeable (0-4)	5 (26%)	16 (25%)	
Satisfactory (5-6)	8 (42%)	29 (45%)	
Knowledgeable (7-8)	6 (32%)	19 (30%)	
Question Item	**Family affected n = 22**	**Family unaffected n = 63**	
"I believe I am knowledgeable about Autism"			0.7639
Agree	9 (41%)	20 (32%)	
Disagree	2 (9%)	6 (10%)	
Neutral	11 (50%)	37 (59%)	
"Autism is a life-long developmental condition"			0.4617
True	16 (73%)	51 (81%)	
False	1 (5%)	1 (2%)	
Not Sure	5 (23%)	11 (17%)	
"Autism can be caused by poor parenting or parental behavior"			0.1510
True	0 (0%)	3 (5%)	
False	17 (77%)	55 (87%)	
Not Sure	5 (23%)	5 (8%)	

Question Item	**Family affected n = 22**	**Family unaffected n = 63**	
"The prevalence of Autism has increased over the years"			0.4242
True	17 (77%)	39 (62%)	
False	0 (0%)	4 (6%)	
Not Sure	5 (23%)	20 (32%)	
"Autism can arise from vaccinations"			0.9007
True	1 (5%)	3 (5%)	
False	17 (77%)	46 (73%)	
Not Sure	4 (18%)	14 (22%)	
"Individuals with Autism always prefer to be alone"			0.1263
True	3 (14%)	4 (6%)	
False	19 (86%)	51 (81%)	
Not Sure	0 (0%)	8 (13%)	
"People with Autism are eccentric geniuses"			0.2341
True	5 (23%)	5 (8%)	
False	12 (55%)	40 (63%)	
Not Sure	5 (23%)	18 (29%)	
"Individuals with Autism can grow out of it"			0.2231
True	3 (14%)	3 (5%)	
False	10 (45%)	38 (60%)	
Not Sure	9 (41%)	22 (35%)	
"People with Autism require substantial medical assistance"			0.8509
True	4 (18%)	14 (22%)	
False	12 (55%)	30 (48%)	
Not Sure	6 (27%)	19 (30%)	
Knowledge Score			0.6318
Not Knowledgeable (0-4)	7 (32%)	15 (24%)	
Satisfactory (5-6)	8 (36%)	30 (48%)	
Knowledgeable (7-8)	7 (32%)	18 (29%)	
Question Item	**Friend affected n = 38**	**Friend unaffected n = 47**	
"I believe I am knowledgeable about Autism"			0.1244
Agree	17 (45%)	12 (26%)	
Disagree	4 (11%)	4 (9%)	
Neutral	17 (45%)	31 (66%)	

Table 3. (Continued)

Question Item	**Friend affected n = 38**	**Friend unaffected n = 47**	
"Autism is a life-long developmental condition"			0.5712
True	30 (79%)	37 (79%)	
False	0 (0%)	2 (4%)	
Not Sure	8 (21%)	8 (17%)	
"Autism can be caused by poor parenting or parental behavior"			0.0420
True	1 (3%)	2 (4%)	
False	29 (76%)	43 (91%)	
Not Sure	8 (21%)	2 (4%)	
"The prevalence of Autism has increased over the years"			0.6880
True	23 (61%)	33 (70%)	
False	2 (5%)	2 (4%)	
Not Sure	13 (34%)	12 (26%)	
"Autism can arise from vaccinations"			0.1641
True	3 (8%)	1 (2%)	
False	30 (79%)	33 (70%)	
Not Sure	5 (13%)	13 (28%)	
"Individuals with Autism always prefer to be alone"			0.0610
True	6 (16%)	1 (2%)	
False	28 (74%)	42 (89%)	
Not Sure	4 (11%)	4 (9%)	
"People with Autism are eccentric geniuses"			0.0221
True	8 (21%)	2 (4%)	
False	18 (47%)	34 (72%)	
Not Sure	12 (32%)	11 (23%)	
"Individuals with Autism can grow out of it"			0.4306
True	4 (11%)	2 (4%)	
False	19 (50%)	29 (62%)	
Not Sure	15 (39%)	16 (34%)	

Question Item	**Friend affected n = 38**	**Friend unaffected n = 47**	
"People with Autism require substantial medical assistance"			0.0557
True	12 (32%)	6 (13%)	
False	14 (37%)	28 (60%)	
Not Sure	12 (32%)	13 (28%)	
Knowledge Score			0.0324
Not Knowledgeable (0-4)	15 (39%)	7 (15%)	
Satisfactory (5-6)	15 (39%)	23 (49%)	
Knowledgeable (7-8)	8 (21%)	17 (36%)	

There was a trend that males were more likely to believe they were knowledgeable - 53% compared to 30% (p=0.0868). There was no actual difference in knowledge (p=0.9999); 32% of males and 30% of females were knowledgeable. 89% and 77% responded in the affirmative to the statement that ASD is a lifelong developmental condition (p=0.7033), and 74% and 64% for the statement that the disorder has increased over the years (p=0.7347). 89% and 86% answered in the negative to the statement that it can be caused by parenting (p=0.4119), 74% and 77% that it can be caused by vaccinations (p=0.4150), 79% and 84% to the statement that ASD individuals prefer to be alone (p=0.5678), 47% and 42% that individuals are eccentric geniuses (p=0.2338), 53% and 59% that individuals can grow out of it (p=0.8395) and 53% and 50% that patients require substantial medical assistance (p=0.5790). (see Table 3).

Those with and without a family member affected by ASD had similar perceptual and actual awareness. 41% of those with a family member affected and 32% of those without one believed they were knowledgeable about ASD (p=0.7639). 73% and 81% answered that it is a lifelong developmental condition (p=0.4617), 77% and 87% remarked that it is not caused by poor parenting (p=0.1510), and 77% and 62% answered that the prevalence has increased over the years (p=0.4242). 77% and 73% noted that vaccinations cannot cause ASD (p=0.9007), 86% and 81% indicated that individuals do not always prefer to be alone (p=0.1263), and 55% and 63% answered that ASD individuals are not all eccentric geniuses (p=0.2341). 45% and 60% concluded that one cannot grow out of ASD (p=0.2231), and 55% and 48% noted that affected individuals do not require substantial medical assistance (p=0.8509). 32% and 29% were deemed knowledgeable (p=0.6318) (see Table 3).

Those with friends affected by ASD were less knowledgeable (21% vs 36%; p=0.0324), while perceived awareness trended towards the other direction (45% vs 26%; p=0.1244). 79% of both groups remarked that it is a lifelong developmental condition (p=0.5712). 76% and 91% remarked that it cannot be caused by poor parenting (p=0.0420). 61% and 70% indicated that it has increased over the years (p=0.6880). 79% and 70% answered that vaccinations cannot cause ASD (p=0.1641). 74% and 89% noted that individuals with ASD do not always prefer to be alone (p=0.0610). 47% and 72% noted that individuals with ASD are not eccentric geniuses (p=0.0221). 50% compared to 62% noted that patients can grow out of it (p=0.4306), and 37% compared to 60% remarked that it patients do not require substantial medical assistance (p=0.0557) (see Table 3).

DISCUSSION

26% of respondents reported having a family member affected by ASD, and 45% described having a friend with ASD. These rates are similar to those previously studied in London, Canada (8). The awareness rate of 29% was higher than the proportion of individuals with family members affected by ASD but lower than the proportion of individuals with friends affected. The results indicate that awareness may be a result of exposure to family members with ASD, as opposed to exposure to friends (as suggested in London) (8).

The discrepancy between perceived awareness (34%) and actual awareness (29%) was lower than the rates detailed in London - 54% and 56%, respectively. The data also suggests that perceived awareness is greater than actual awareness, which is contrary to young adults in London with respect to ASD and also for young adults with respect to other diseases such as Alzheimer's and Parkinson's disease (9-14).

The data also indicates that awareness level is lower than the percentage of individuals with friends affected by ASD. This may suggest that future ASD diagnoses may fall within this population, but further longitudinal studies should investigate into such an inference.

This study was not without limitations. As it is a survey study, there exists the possibility of a sampling and response bias. The large sample size hopefully would normalize the data and reduce the effect size of any anomalies/outliers.

In conclusion, 29% were aware of ASD, which is lower than the perceived awareness level of 34%. The awareness level is greater than the percentage of individuals with family members affected by ASD (26%) but lower than the percentage of individuals with friends affected by ASD (45%). This suggests that exposure to family, and not friends, may contribute a greater role to ASD awareness.

REFERENCES

[1] Chakrabarti S, Fombonne E. Pervasive developmental disorders in preschool children. JAMA 2001;285:3093-9.

[2] Chakrabarti S, Fombonne E. Pervasive development disorders in preschool children: confirmation of high prevalence. Am J Psychiatry 2005;162:1133-41.

[3] Bertrand J, Mars A, Boyle C, Bove F, Yeargin-Allsop M, DeCoufle P. Prevalence of autism in a United States population: the Brick Township, New Jersey, investigation. Pediatrics 2001;108:1155-61.

[4] Yeargin-Allsop M, Rice C, Karapurkar T, Doernberg N, Boyle C, Murphy C. Prevalence of autism in a US metropolitan area. JAMA 2003;289:49-55.

[5] Fombonne E, Zakarian R, Bennett A, Meng L, McLean-Heywood D. Pervasive developmental disorders in Montreal, Quebec, Canada: prevalence and links with immunization. Pediatrics 2006;118:e139-50.

[6] Shattuck PT. The combination of diagnostic substitution to the growing administrative prevalence of autism in US special education data. Pediatrics 2006;117:1028-37.

[7] Chow R, Viehweger J. Are young adults aware of autism spectrum disorder? Int Public Health J 2019;11(1), in press.

[8] Chow R, Viehweger J, Anpalagan T, Yang H, Banerjee R. Awareness of Autism Spectrum Disorder among young adults in London, Canada. Int Public Health J 2019;11(1), in press.

[9] Chow R, Viehweger J, Trasente V, Borean M, Hollenberg D, Lam M, et al. Awareness of Parkinson's disease among young adults in London, Canada. J Pain Manage 2019;12(1), in press.

[10] Ho S, Viehweger J, Trasente V, Ho C, Ng W, Wong M et al. Awareness of Parkinson's disease among young adults in Toronto, Canada. J Pain Manage 2019;12(1), in press.

[11] Viehweger J, Chow R, Trasente V, Duarte N, Borean M, Hollenberg D et al. Awareness of Parkinson's disease among young adults in Waterloo, Canada. J Pain Manage 2019;12(1), in press.

[12] Chow R, Ferrara A, Borean M, Hollenberg D, Lam M, Anpalagan T, et al. Awareness of Alzheimer's disease among young adults in London, Canada. Int J Child Health Hum Dev 2018; in press.

[13] Chow R, Borean M, Hollenberg D, Midroni L, Midroni C, Kim Y, et al. Awareness of Alzheimer's disease among young adults in Kingston, Canada. Int J Child Health Hum Dev 2018; in press.

[14] Borean M, Rzepka A, Trasente V, Hollenberg D, Ho C, Ng W, et al. Awareness of Alzheimer's disease among young adults in Toronto, Canada. Int J Child Health Hum Dev 2018; in press.

[15] Chow R, Viehweger J. Assessing awareness of Autism Spectrum Disorder: about the survey instrument. Int Public Health J 2019;11(1), in press.

In: Autism Spectrum Disorder ISBN: 978-1-53612-730-0
Editors: R. Chow, J. Viehweger et al. ©2017 Nova Science Publishers, Inc.

Chapter 5

AWARENESS OF AUTISM SPECTRUM DISORDER AMONG YOUNG ADULTS IN MONTREAL, CANADA

Jaclyn Viehweger, BMSc(C), Ronald Chow*, BMSc(C) and Michael Borean, BMSc(C)
Infinitas Research Group, London, Ontario, Canada

The aim of this chapter was to report the awareness of young adults in Montreal, Canada, with respect to autism spectrum disorder (ASD). Descriptive statistics were used to convey participant demographics, and also the responses provided by participants. Fisher exact tests were run to investigate whether different subgroups provided different responses. Subgroup analyses were conducted by age group (under/over 20 years old), sex (males/females), whether they have a family member with ASD, and whether they have a friend with ASD. A total of 31 participants consented and completed the questionnaire. 39% identified that they were between 20 and 22 years old, 26% were over 22 years old, 23% were between 18 and 19 years old, and 4 were under 18 years old. 3% did not identify their sex, 10% were male, and the remaining (87%) were female. 39% knew of a family member affected by ASD, and 71% knew of a friend affected by ASD. 55% of young adults in Montreal were aware of

* Correspondence: Ronald Chow BMSc(C), Infinitas Research Group, London, Ontario, Canada. Email: rchow48@uwo.ca.

the disease. This proportion is higher than the 39% who have a family member with ASD and lower than the 71% who know of a friend affected by ASD. This data is in-line with prior studies, and that awareness may be greater correlated to exposure to family members with ASD. Future prevalence of ASD may be similar but future longitudinal studies should further investigate.

INTRODUCTION

The awareness of autism spectrum disorder (ASD) has been suggested to be a precursor to the prevalence of ASD (1-3). Hence, looking into the awareness of ASD among today's youth may allow researchers to predict the number of diagnoses that will occur in the near future (3).

Chow et al. published an original study investigating young adults in London, Canada (4). 26% had a family member affected by ASD, and 44% had a friend afflicted by ASD. 56% were aware of ASD, indicating that awareness exceeds the current prevalence of ASD; future prevalence of ASD may be greater than today (4).

Two follow-up studies were conducted by Chow et al. of young adults in Toronto (Canada) (5) and California (United States of America) (6). In Toronto, 29% were aware of ASD, 26% had family members were affected and 34% had a friend affected. The results suggest that exposure to family members with ASD may contribute to greater awareness, and that future prevalence may be approximately equal (5). For young adults in California, 50% were knowledgeable, while 50% had a family member affected and 71% had a friend with ASD. The data here supports the study looking into young adults in Toronto, and similarly reported that future prevalence may be similar (6).

The two follow-up studies had a different conclusion than the original study in London. There was also tremendous variation between the three published studies. The aim of our paper was to report the awareness of young adults in Montreal, Canada, with respect to ASD.

OUR STUDY

A three-page survey was sent to young adults in the Montreal. The first page had a consent form listing the benefits/costs, and required participants to consent in order to complete the questionnaire. The second page collected participant demographics, and the third page assessed the perceived knowledge of ASD and also contained eight assessment questions (7).

Descriptive statistics were used to convey participant demographics, and also the responses provided by participants. Fisher exact tests were run to investigate whether different subgroups provided different responses. Subgroup analyses were conducted by age group (under/over 20 years old), sex (males/females), whether they have a family member with ASD, and whether they have a friend with ASD. P-values less than 0.05 were considered statistically significant. All statistical procedures were conducted using the Statistical Analysis Software (SAS Version 9.4 for Windows) (7).

FINDINGS

A total of 31 participants consented and completed the questionnaire. 39% identified that they were between 20 and 22 years old, 26% were over 22 years old, 23% were between 18 and 19 years old, and 4 were under 18 years old. 3% did not identify their sex, 10% were male, and the remaining (87%) were female. 39% knew of a family member affected by ASD, and 71% knew of a friend affected by ASD (see Table 1).

55% believed they were knowledgeable about ASD. 84%, 90% and 52% remarked that ASD is a lifelong developmental condition, that it is not caused by poor parenting, and that its prevalence has increased over the years. 97%, 84%, 81% and 74% answered that it does not arise from vaccinations, individuals do not always prefer to be alone, patients are not all eccentric geniuses, and that affected individuals do not grow out of it. 55% responded that patients do not require substantial medical assistance.

19% were not knowledgeable, 33% had satisfactory knowledge, and 48% were knowledgeable (see Table 2).

When comparing the eleven adults under 20 years old and 20 above 20 years old, no difference was found in perceptual and actual awareness. 36% and 65% of the two groups, respectively, believed they were knowledgeable (p = 0.3341); 18% and 20% were actually knowledgeable (p = 0.9999). 91% and 80% correctly noted that it is a lifelong developmental condition (p = 0.9999), 100% and 85% that it is not caused by poor parenting (p = 0.5350), 36% and 60% that its prevalence has increased over the years (p = 0.3024), and 91% and 100% that it is not a result of vaccinations (p = 0.3548). 0% and 5% incorrectly concluded that individuals prefer to be alone (p = 0.7491), 18% and 5% that not all ASD people are eccentric geniuses (p = 0.5512), 9% and 10% that individuals can grow out of it (p = 0.8263) and 18% and 10% that individuals require substantial medical assistance (p = 0.7670). 45% of the younger and 50% of the older cohort were knowledgeable (p = 0.9999) (see Table 3).

Table 1. Demographics

Demographic	**n = 31**
Age Group	
Under 18 years old	4 (12%)
18-19 years old	7 (23%)
20-22 years old	12 (39%)
Over 22 years old	8 (26%)
Sex	
Male	3 (10%)
Female	27 (87%)
Prefer not to say	1 (3%)
Family member affected by Autism	
Yes	12 (39%)
No	19 (61%)
Friend(s) affected by Autism	
Yes	22 (71%)
No	9 (29%)

Table 2. Perceived and actual knowledge

Question Item	**n = 31**
"I believe I am knowledgeable about Autism"	
Agree	17 (55%)
Disagree	4 (13%)
Neutral	10 (32%)
"Autism is a life-long developmental condition"	
True	26 (84%)
False	1 (3%)
Not Sure	4 (13%)
"Autism can be caused by poor parenting or parental behavior"	
True	0 (0%)
False	28 (90%)
Not Sure	3 (10%)
"The prevalence of Autism has increased over the years"	
True	16 (52%)
False	4 (13%)
Not Sure	11 (35%)
"Autism can arise from vaccinations"	
True	0 (0%)
False	30 (97%)
Not Sure	1 (3%)
"Individuals with Autism always prefer to be alone"	
True	1 (3%)
False	26 (84%)
Not Sure	4 (13%)
"People with Autism are eccentric geniuses"	
True	3 (10%)
False	25 (81%)
Not Sure	3 (10%)
"Individuals with Autism can grow out of it"	
True	3 (10%)
False	23 (74%)
Not Sure	5 (16%)
"People with Autism require substantial medical assistance"	
True	4 (13%)
False	17 (55%)
Not Sure	10 (33%)
Knowledge Score	
Not Knowledgeable (0-4)	6 (19%)
Satisfactory (5-6)	10 (33%)
Knowledgeable (7-8)	15 (48%)

Table 3. Perceived and actual knowledge - by subgroups

Question Item	Under 20 n = 11	Over 20 n = 20	p-value
"I believe I am knowledgeable about Autism"			0.3341
Agree	4 (36%)	13 (65%)	
Disagree	2 (18%)	2 (10%)	
Neutral	5 (56%)	5 (25%)	
"Autism is a life-long developmental condition"			0.9999
True	10 (91%)	16 (80%)	
False	0 (0%)	1 (5%)	
Not Sure	1 (9%)	3 (15%)	
"Autism can be caused by poor parenting or parental behavior"			0.5350
True	0 (0%)	0 (0%)	
False	11 (100%)	17 (85%)	
Not Sure	0 (0%)	3 (15%)	
"The prevalence of Autism has increased over the years"			0.3024
True	4 (36%)	12 (60%)	
False	1 (9%)	3 (15%)	
Not Sure	6 (55%)	5 (25%)	
"Autism can arise from vaccinations"			0.3548
True	0 (0%)	0 (0%)	
False	10 (91%)	20 (100%)	
Not Sure	1 (9%)	0 (0%)	
"Individuals with Autism always prefer to be alone"			0.7491
True	0 (0%)	1 (5%)	
False	9 (82%)	17 (85%)	
Not Sure	2 (18%)	2 (10%)	
"People with Autism are eccentric geniuses"			0.5512
True	2 (18%)	1 (5%)	
False	8 (73%)	17 (85%)	
Not Sure	1 (9%)	2 (10%)	
"Individuals with Autism can grow out of it"			0.8263
True	1 (9%)	2 (10%)	
False	9 (82%)	14 (70%)	
Not Sure	1 (9%)	4 (20%)	

Question Item	**Under 20** **n = 11**	**Over 20** **n = 20**	**p-value**
"People with Autism require substantial medical assistance"			0.7670
True	2 (18%)	2 (10%)	
False	6 (55%)	11 (55%)	
Not Sure	3 (27%)	7 (35%)	
Knowledge Score			0.9999
Not Knowledgeable (0-4)	2 (18%)	4 (20%)	
Satisfactory (5-6)	4 (36%)	6 (30%)	
Knowledgeable (7-8)	5 (45%)	10 (50%)	
Question Item	**Family affected** **n = 12**	**Family unaffected** **n = 19**	
"I believe I am knowledgeable about Autism"			0.0455
Agree	10 (83%)	7 (37%)	
Disagree	0 (0%)	4 (21%)	
Neutral	2 (17%)	8 (42%)	
"Autism is a life-long developmental condition"			0.1832
True	12 (100%)	14 (74%)	
False	0 (0%)	1 (5%)	
Not Sure	0 (0%)	4 (21%)	
"Autism can be caused by poor parenting or parental behavior"			0.5435
True	0 (0%)	0 (0%)	
False	10 (83%)	18 (95%)	
Not Sure	2 (17%)	1 (5%)	
"The prevalence of Autism has increased over the years"			0.5097
True	8 (67%)	8 (42%)	
False	1 (8%)	3 (16%)	
Not Sure	3 (25%)	8 (42%)	
"Autism can arise from vaccinations"			0.9999
True	0 (0%)	0 (0%)	
False	12 (100%)	18 (95%)	
Not Sure	0 (0%)	1 (5%)	
"Individuals with Autism always prefer to be alone"			0.5552
True	1 (8%)	0 (0%)	
False	10 (83%)	16 (84%)	
Not Sure	1 (8%)	3 (16%)	

Table 3. (Continued)

Question Item	**Family affected n = 12**	**Family unaffected n = 19**	
"People with Autism are eccentric geniuses"			0.9999
True	1 (8%)	2 (11%)	
False	10 (83%)	15 (79%)	
Not Sure	1 (8%)	2 (11%)	
"Individuals with Autism can grow out of it"			0.9999
True	1 (8%)	2 (11%)	
False	9 (75%)	14 (74%)	
Not Sure	2 (17%)	3 (16%)	
"People with Autism require substantial medical assistance"			0.4371
True	2 (17%)	2 (11%)	
False	8 (67%)	9 (47%)	
Not Sure	2 (17%)	8 (42%)	
Knowledge Score			0.2793
Not Knowledgeable (0-4)	2 (17%)	4 (21%)	
Satisfactory (5-6)	2 (17%)	8 (42%)	
Knowledgeable (7-8)	8 (67%)	7 (37%)	
Question Item	**Friend affected n = 22**	**Friend unaffected n = 9**	
"I believe I am knowledgeable about Autism"			0.2936
Agree	14 (64%)	3 (33%)	
Disagree	2 (9%)	2 (22%)	
Neutral	6 (27%)	4 (44%)	
"Autism is a life-long developmental condition"			0.0627
True	20 (91%)	6 (67%)	
False	1 (5%)	0 (0%)	
Not Sure	1 (5%)	3 (33%)	
"Autism can be caused by poor parenting or parental behavior"			0.5375
True	0 (0%)	0 (0%)	
False	19 (86%)	9 (100%)	
Not Sure	3 (14%)	0 (0%)	
"The prevalence of Autism has increased over the years"			0.0074
True	13 (59%)	3 (33%)	
False	0 (0%)	4 (44%)	
Not Sure	9 (41%)	2 (22%)	

Question Item	**Friend affected n = 22**	**Friend unaffected n = 9**	
"Autism can arise from vaccinations"			0.2903
True	0 (0%)	0 (0%)	
False	22 (100%)	8 (89%)	
Not Sure	0 (0%)	1 (11%)	
"Individuals with Autism always prefer to be alone"			0.6900
True			
False	1 (5%)	0 (0%)	
Not Sure	19 (86%)	7 (78%)	
	2 (9%)	2 (22%)	
"People with Autism are eccentric geniuses"			0.2040
True	1 (5%)	2 (22%)	
False	18 (82%)	7 (78%)	
Not Sure	3 (14%)	0 (0%)	
"Individuals with Autism can grow out of it"			0.6674
True	3 (14%)	0 (0%)	
False	16 (73%)	7 (78%)	
Not Sure	3 (14%)	2 (22%)	
"People with Autism require substantial medical assistance"			0.1757
True	3 (14%)	1 (11%)	
False	14 (64%)	3 (33%)	
Not Sure	5 (23%)	5 (56%)	
Knowledge Score			0.1696
Not Knowledgeable (0-4)	3 (14%)	3 (33%)	
Satisfactory (5-6)	6 (27%)	4 (44%)	
Knowledgeable (7-8)	13 (59%)	2 (22%)	

Those with affected family members perceived themselves as more knowledgeable (83% compared to 37%; $p = 0.0455$), and actual knowledge did not differ between the groups (67% compared to 37%; $p = 0.2793$). 100% and 74%, and 67% and 42% remarked in the affirmative to the following two statements, respectively: "Autism is a lifelong developmental condition" ($p = 0.1832$) and "the prevalence of autism has increased over the years" ($p = 0.5097$). The following questions were answered in the negative form by the following proportions: 83% and 95% for "Autism can be caused by poor parenting or parental behavior" ($p = 0.5435$), 100% and 95% to "Autism can arise from vaccinations" (p = 0.9999), 83% and 84% to “Individuals with autism always prefer to be alone” (p = 0.5552), 83% and 79% to “People with autism are eccentric geniuses” (p = 0.9999), 75% and 74% to “Individuals with autism can grow out of it” (p = 0.9999), and 67% and 47% to “People with autism require substantial medical assistance” (p = 0.4371) (see Table 3).

No difference was found with respect to awareness between those with and without affected friends. 64% and 33% noted that those with and without affected friends, respectively, believe they are knowledgeable (p = 0.2936). 91% and 67% remarked that ASD is a lifelong developmental condition (p = 0.0627), and 59% and 33% indicated that the prevalence has increased over the years (p = 0.0074). 86% and 100% noted that ASD cannot be caused by poor parenting, and 100% and 89% concluded that it cannot arise from vaccinations (p = 0.2903). 86% and 78% responded that individuals do not prefer to be alone (p = 0.6900), and 82% and 78% voiced that not all individuals are eccentric geniuses (p = 0.2040). 73% and 78% remarked that individuals cannot grow out of it (p = 0.6674), and 64% and 33% noted that not all patients require substantial medical assistance (p = 0.1757). Overall, 59% and 22% were knowledgeable about ASD (p = 0.1696) (see Table 3).

DISCUSSION

A much larger proportion of young adults know of a friend affected by ASD (71%), as opposed to a family member with ASD (39%). The perceived awareness (55%) was slightly higher than the actual awareness (48%). The interpretation from this data is similar to two previously published studies (5-6) - the awareness may be greater correlated to exposure to family members with ASD, and that future prevalence may be approximately similar.

Subgroup analyses indicates that demographic information does not seem to be correlated with greater awareness of ASD - age, exposure to family members, and exposure to friends does not seem to increase the knowledge of the disease.

This study was not without limitations. As it is a survey study, there exists the possibility of a response and sampling bias. The sample size hopefully normalized any anomalies/outliers.

In conclusion, 55% of young adults in Montreal were aware of the disease. This proportion is higher than the 39% who have a family member with ASD and lower than the 71% who know of a friend affected by ASD. This data is in-line with prior studies, and that awareness may be greater correlated to exposure to family members with ASD. Future prevalence of ASD may be similar but future longitudinal studies should further investigate.

ACKNOWLEDGMENTS

We would like to thank Tharani Anpalagan for the support.

REFERENCES

[1] Fombonne E, Zakarian R, Bennett A, Meng L, McLean-Heywood D. Pervasive developmental disorders in Montreal, Quebec, Canada: Prevalence and links with immunization. Pediatrics 2006;118:e139-50.

[2] Shattuck PT. The combination of diagnostic substitution to the growing administrative prevalence of autism in US special education data. Pediatrics 2006;117:1028-37.

[3] Chow R, Viehweger J, Merrick J. Are young adults aware of autism spectrum disorder? Int Public Health J 2019;11(1), in press.

[4] Chow R, Viehweger J, Anpalagan T, Yang H, Banerjee R. Awareness of autism spectrum disorder among young adults in London, Canada. Int Public Health J 2019;11(1), in press.

[5] Chow R, Viehweger J, Hollenberg D, Ho C, Ng W, Wong M. Awareness of autism spectrum disorder among young adults in Toronto, Canada. Int Public Health J 2019;11(1), in press.

[6] Chow R, Viehweger J, Murai A. Awareness of autism spectrum disorder among young adults in California, USA. Int Public Health J 2019;11(1), in press.

[7] Chow R, Viehweger J. Assessing awareness of autism spectrum disorder: About the survey instrument. Int Public Health J 2019;11(1), in press.

In: Autism Spectrum Disorder ISBN: 978-1-53612-730-0
Editors: R. Chow, J. Viehweger et al. ©2017 Nova Science Publishers, Inc.

Chapter 6

AWARENESS OF AUTISM SPECTRUM DISORDER AMONG YOUNG ADULTS IN CALGARY, CANADA

Ronald Chow*, BMSc(C)
and Jaclyn Viehweger, BMSc(C)
Infinitas Research Group, London, Ontario, Canada

Research has been conducted to evaluate the awareness of young adults with respect to autism spectrum disorder (ASD), as it has been suggested that awareness is positively correlated with the number of diagnoses. There exists a discrepancy in conclusion between the published studies. Additionally, there seems to exist tremendous variation. The aim of our study was to evaluate the awareness of young adults in Calgary, Canada. A three-page survey was sent to young adults in Calgary. 53% were knowledgeable about ASD. 43% have a family member affected with ASD, and 67% have a friend affected by ASD. These results suggest that exposure to family members may be a significant determinant of awareness. It may also suggest that future prevalence may be similar to current prevalence, although longitudinal studies should investigate whether this observation perpetuates in the subsequent decades.

---

* Correspondence: Ronald Chow BMSc(C), Infinitas Research Group, London, Ontario, Canada. Email: rchow48@uwo.ca.

INTRODUCTION

Research has been conducted to evaluate the awareness of young adults with respect to autism spectrum disorder (ASD), as it has been suggested that awareness is positively correlated with the number of diagnoses (1, 2). The original study in London, Canada (3), remarked that 56% were aware of ASD, which is higher than the proportion of individuals with a family member (26%) and friend (44%) affected by ASD. The data suggests that future prevalence may be greater than today.

Follow-up studies conducted in Toronto (4), California (5) and Montreal (6) suggested that future prevalence may be similar to today's prevalence. In Toronto, 29% were aware of the disease, while 26% of family members were affected and 34% of friends were affected. In California, 50% were knowledgeable, 50% had a family member and 71% had a friend afflicted. In Montreal, 55% were knowledgeable, 39% had a family member affected, and 71% knew of a friend with ASD.

There exists a discrepancy in conclusion between the published studies. Additionally, there seems to exist tremendous variation. The aim of our study was to evaluate the awareness of young adults in Calgary, Canada.

OUR SURVEY

A three-page survey was sent to young adults in Calgary. The first page had a consent form listing the benefits/costs, and required participants to consent in order to complete the questionnaire. The second page collected participant demographics, and the third page assessed the perceived knowledge of ASD and also contained eight assessment questions (7).

Descriptive statistics were used to convey participant demographics, and also the responses provided by participants. Fisher exact tests were run to investigate whether different subgroups provided different responses. Subgroup analyses were conducted by age group (under/over 20 years old), sex (males/females), whether they have a family member with ASD, and whether they have a friend with ASD. P-values less than 0.05 were considered statistically significant. All statistical procedures were conducted using the Statistical Analysis Software (SAS Version 9.4 for Windows) (7).

FINDINGS

Thirty participants consented and completed the questionnaire. The largest proportion of participants (40%) indicated they were between 18 and 19 years old, 27% noted they were between 20 and 22 years old, 23% responded they were over 22 years old, and 10% answered that they were under 18 years old. 87% of respondents were female, 10% were male, and 3% did not identify their sex. 43% had a family member affected by ASD, and 67% had a friend affected by ASD (see Table 1).

63% believed they were knowledgeable about ASD. 93% and 90% noted that ASD is a lifelong developmental condition and it is not caused by poor parenting. 63% answered that the prevalence has increased over the years, and 30% that it cannot arise from vaccinations. 80%, 73%, 80% and 53% answered “False” to the following statements, respectively: “Individuals with autism always prefer to be alone,” “People with autism are eccentric geniuses,” “Individuals with autism can grow out of it,” and “People with autism require substantial medical assistance.” 53% were knowledgeable about ASD - they received a score of 7 or 8 out of 8 (see Table 2).

Half of the respondents were under 20 years old, and the other half were over 20 years old. Perceived and actual awareness did not differ between the two age cohorts. 53% and 73% believed they were knowledgeable ($p = 0.4497$), for the two groups respectively. 47% and 60% were actually knowledgeable ($p = 0.6051$). 93% of both groups answered in the affirmative that ASD is a lifelong developmental condition ($p = 0.9999$), and 47% and 80% that its prevalence has increased over the years ($p = 0.1086$). 93% and 87% noted that it is not caused by poor parenting ($p = 0.4828$), 87% and 93% that it cannot arise from vaccinations (p = 0.7414), 87% and 73% that ASD individuals do not all prefer to be alone (p = 0.6621) and 73% of both groups that they are not eccentric geniuses (p = 0.9999). 87% and 73% answered that ASD individuals do not grow out of it (p = 0.6621), and 40% and 67% that patients do not require substantial medical assistance (p = 0.1668). 47% and 60% were knowledgeable (p = 0.6051) (see Table 3).

There was also no difference in perceived (p = 0.0846) and actual (p = 0.3267) awareness between those with and without family members affected by ASD. No difference in response was found in any specific assessment question: "Autism is a lifelong developmental condition" (p = 0.9999), "Autism can be caused by poor parenting or parental behavior" (p = 0.1793), "The prevalence of autism has increased over the years" (p = 0.8410), "Autism can arise from vaccinations" (p = 0.9999), "Individuals with autism always prefer to be alone" (p = 0.9999), "People with Autism are eccentric geniuses" (p = 0.8380), "Individuals with autism can grow out of it" (p = 0.4214), and "People with autism require substantial medical assistance" (p = 0.3267) (see Table 3).

Table 1. Demographics

Demographic	**n = 30**
Age Group	
Under 18 years old	3 (10%)
18-19 years old	12 (40%)
20-22 years old	8 (27%)
Over 22 years old	7 (23%)
Sex	
Male	3 (10%)
Female	26 (87%)
Prefer not to say	1 (3%)
Family member affected by Autism	
Yes	13 (43%)
No	17 (57%)
Friend(s) affected by Autism	
Yes	20 (67%)
No	10 (33%)

Table 2. Perceived and actual knowledge

Question Item	n = 30
"I believe I am knowledgeable about Autism"	
Agree	19 (63%)
Disagree	1 (3%)
Neutral	10 (33%)
"Autism is a life-long developmental condition"	
True	28 (93%)
False	1 (3%)
Not Sure	1 (3%)
"Autism can be caused by poor parenting or parental behavior"	
True	1 (3%)
False	27 (90%)
Not Sure	2 (7%)
"The prevalence of Autism has increased over the years"	
True	19 (63%)
False	2 (7%)
Not Sure	9 (30%)
"Autism can arise from vaccinations"	
True	1 (3%)
False	27 (30%)
Not Sure	2 (7%)
"Individuals with Autism always prefer to be alone"	
True	4 (13%)
False	24 (80%)
Not Sure	2 (7%)
"People with Autism are eccentric geniuses"	
True	3 (10%)
False	22 (73%)
Not Sure	5 (17%)
"Individuals with Autism can grow out of it"	
True	2 (7%)
False	24 (80%)
Not Sure	4 (13%)
"People with Autism require substantial medical assistance"	
True	5 (17%)
False	16 (53%)
Not Sure	9 (30%)
Knowledge Score	
Not Knowledgeable (0-4)	5 (17%)
Satisfactory (5-6)	9 (30%)
Knowledgeable (7-8)	16 (53%)

Table 3. Perceived and actual knowledge - by subgroups

Question Item	Under 20 n = 15	Over 20 n = 15	p-value
"I believe I am knowledgeable about Autism"			0.4497
Agree	8 (53%)	11 (73%)	
Disagree	1 (7%)	0 (0%)	
Neutral	6 (40%)	4 (27%)	
"Autism is a life-long developmental condition"			0.9999
True	14 (93%)	14 (93%)	
False	0 (0%)	1 (7%)	
Not Sure	1 (7%)	0 (0%)	
"Autism can be caused by poor parenting or parental behavior"			0.4828
True	1 (7%)	0 (0%)	
False	14 (93%)	13 (87%)	
Not Sure	0 (0%)	2 (13%)	
"The prevalence of Autism has increased over the years"			0.1086
True	7 (47%)	12 (80%)	
False	1 (7%)	1 (7%)	
Not Sure	7 (47%)	2 (13%)	
"Autism can arise from vaccinations"			0.7414
True	1 (7%)	0 (0%)	
False	13 (87%)	14 (93%)	
Not Sure	1 (7%)	1 (7%)	
"Individuals with Autism always prefer to be alone"			0.6621
True	1 (7%)	3 (20%)	
False	13 (87%)	11 (73%)	
Not Sure	1 (7%)	1 (7%)	
"People with Autism are eccentric geniuses"			0.9999
True	1 (7%)	2 (13%)	
False	11 (73%)	11 (73%)	
Not Sure	3 (20%)	2 (13%)	
"Individuals with Autism can grow out of it"			0.6621
True	1 (7%)	1 (7%)	
False	13 (87%)	11 (73%)	
Not Sure	1 (7%)	3 (20%)	

Question Item	**Under 20 n = 15**	**Over 20 n = 15**	**p-value**
"People with Autism require substantial medical assistance"			0.1668
True	2 (13%)	3 (20%)	
False	6 (40%)	10 (67%)	
Not Sure	7 (47%)	2 (13%)	
Knowledge Score			0.6051
Not Knowledgeable (0-4)	2 (13%)	3 (20%)	
Satisfactory (5-6)	6 (40%)	3 (20%)	
Knowledgeable (7-8)	7 (47%)	9 (60%)	
Question Item	**Family affected n = 13**	**Family unaffected n = 17**	
"I believe I am knowledgeable about Autism"			0.0846
Agree	11 (85%)	8 (47%)	
Disagree	0 (0%)	1 (6%)	
Neutral	2 (15%)	8 (47%)	
"Autism is a life-long developmental condition"			0.9999
True	13 (100%)	15 (88%)	
False	0 (0%)	1 (6%)	
Not Sure	0 (0%)	1 (6%)	
"Autism can be caused by poor parenting or parental behavior"			0.1793
True	0 (0%)	1 (6%)	
False	11 (85%)	16 (94%)	
Not Sure	2 (15%)	0 (0%)	
"The prevalence of Autism has increased over the years"			0.8410
True	9 (69%)	10 (59%)	
False	1 (8%)	1 (6%)	
Not Sure	3 (23%)	6 (35%)	
"Autism can arise from vaccinations"			0.9999
True	0 (0%)	1 (6%)	
False	12 (92%)	15 (88%)	
Not Sure	1 (8%)	1 (6%)	
"Individuals with Autism always prefer to be alone"			0.9999
True	2 (15%)	2 (12%)	
False	10 (77%)	14 (82%)	
Not Sure	1 (8%)	1 (6%)	

Table 3. (Continued)

Question Item	Family affected n = 13	Family unaffected n = 17	
"People with Autism are eccentric geniuses"			0.8380
True	2 (15%)	1 (6%)	
False	9 (69%)	13 (76%)	
Not Sure	2 (15%)	3 (18%)	
"Individuals with Autism can grow out of it"			0.4214
True	1 (8%)	1 (6%)	
False	9 (69%)	15 (88%)	
Not Sure	3 (23%)	1 (6%)	
"People with Autism require substantial medical assistance"			0.3267
True	3 (23%)	2 (12%)	
False	8 (62%)	8 (47%)	
Not Sure	2 (15%)	7 (41%)	
Knowledge Score			0.3267
Not Knowledgeable (0-4)	3 (23%)	2 (12%)	
Satisfactory (5-6)	2 (15%)	7 (41%)	
Knowledgeable (7-8)	8 (62%)	8 (47%)	
Question Item	**Friend affected n = 20**	**Friend unaffected n = 10**	
"I believe I am knowledgeable about Autism"			0.2900
Agree	14 (70%)	5 (50%)	
Disagree	0 (0%)	1 (10%)	
Neutral	6 (30%)	4 (40%)	
"Autism is a life-long developmental condition"			0.5632
True	19 (95%)	9 (90%)	
False	1 (5%)	0 (0%)	
Not Sure	0 (0%)	1 (10%)	
"Autism can be caused by poor parenting or parental behavior"			0.6880
True	1 (5%)	0 (0%)	
False	17 (85%)	10 (100%)	
Not Sure	2 (10%)	0 (0%)	
"The prevalence of Autism has increased over the years"			0.5867
True	13 (65%)	6 (60%)	
False	2 (10%)	0 (0%)	
Not Sure	5 (25%)	4 (40%)	

Question Item	**Friend affected n = 20**	**Friend unaffected n = 10**	
"Autism can arise from vaccinations"			0.1034
True	1 (5%)	0 (0%)	
False	19 (95%)	8 (80%)	
Not Sure	0 (0%)	2 (20%)	
"Individuals with Autism always prefer to be alone"			0.9999
True	3 (15%)	1 (10%)	
False	16 (80%)	8 (80%)	
Not Sure	1 (5%)	1 (10%)	
"People with Autism are eccentric geniuses"			0.3957
True	1 (5%)	2 (20%)	
False	16 (80%)	6 (60%)	
Not Sure	3 (15%)	2 (20%)	
"Individuals with Autism can grow out of it"			0.1927
True	2 (10%)	0 (0%)	
False	17 (85%)	7 (70%)	
Not Sure	1 (5%)	3 (30%)	
"People with Autism require substantial medical assistance"			0.0136
True	3 (15%)	2 (20%)	
False	14 (70%)	2 (20%)	
Not Sure	3 (15%)	6 (60%)	
Knowledge Score			0.1683
Not Knowledgeable (0-4)	3 (15%)	2 (20%)	
Satisfactory (5-6)	4 (20%)	5 (50%)	
Knowledgeable (7-8)	13 (65%)	3 (30%)	

Respondents with ASD friends were not more knowledgeable than those without ASD friends. 70% and 50%, respectively, believed they were knowledgeable about ASD ($p = 0.2900$). 95% and 90% answered that it is a lifelong developmental condition ($p = 0.5632$); 85% and 100% indicated that it is not caused by poor parenting ($p = 0.6880$); 65% and 60% responded that its prevalence has increased over the years ($p = 0.5867$); 95% and 80% remarked that it is not caused by vaccinations ($p = 0.1034$). 80% of both groups noted that individuals do not prefer to be alone ($p = 0.9999$); 80% and 60% concluded that not all are eccentric geniuses ($p = 0.3957$); 85% and 70% responded that individuals cannot grow out of it (p = 0.1927); 70% and 20% remarked that patients do not require substantial medical assistance (p = 0.0136). Overall, 65% and 30% were knowledgeable (p = 0.1683) (see Table 3).

Discussion

53% of participants were knowledgeable about the disorder, which is a greater proportion than those knowing of a family member with ASD (43%) and a smaller proportion than those knowing of a friend with ASD (67%). This conclusion is in-line with prior studies (4-6), suggesting that future prevalence may be similar to current prevalence. Longitudinal studies should be conducted to determine whether this observation perpetuates in the subsequent decades.

Subgroup analyses indicate that none of the participant demographics serve as a predictor for the awareness level of ASD. This result indicates that ASD awareness is relatively constant across the population, and that the awareness may be a result of environmental factors (i.e., public knowledge and advocacy for greater awareness). The fact that the proportion aware is greater than the proportion with an affected family member suggests that exposure to family members with ASD may be a significant determinant of awareness.

This study was not without limitations. As it is a survey study, there exists the possibility of a response and sampling bias. The sample size of the study hopefully normalized any abnormalities or outliers.

In conclusion, 53% were knowledgeable about ASD. 43% have a family member affected with ASD, and 67% have a friend affected by ASD. These results suggest that exposure to family members may be a significant determinant of awareness. It may also suggest that future prevalence may be similar to current prevalence, although longitudinal studies should investigate whether this observation perpetuates in the subsequent decades.

ACKNOWLEDGMENTS

We would like to thank Michael Borean, Drew Hollenberg, Tharani Anpalagan and Victoria Trasente for their support.

REFERENCES

[1] Fombonne E, Zakarian R, Bennett A, Meng L, McLean-Heywood D. Pervasive developmental disorders in Montreal, Quebec, Canada: Prevalence and links with immunization. Pediatrics 2006;118:e139-50.

[2] Shattuck PT. The combination of diagnostic substitution to the growing administrative prevalence of autism in US special education data. Pediatrics 2006;117:1028-37.

[3] Chow R, Viehweger J, Anpalagan T, Yang H, Banerjee R. Awareness of autism spectrum disorder among young adults in London, Canada. Int Public Health J 2019;11(1), in press.

[4] Chow R, Viehweger J, Hollenberg D, Ho C, Ng W, Wong M. Awareness of autism spectrum disorder among young adults in Toronto, Canada. Int Public Health J 2019;11(1), in press.

[5] Chow R, Viehweger J, Murai A. Awareness of autism spectrum disorder among young adults in California, USA. Int Public Health J 2019;11(1), in press.

[6] Viehweger J, Chow R, Borean M. Awareness of autism spectrum disorder among young adults in Montreal, Canada. Int Public Health J 2019;11(1), in press.

[7] Chow R, Viehweger J. Assessing awareness of autism spectrum disorder: about the survey instrument. Int Public Health J 2019;11(1), in press.

In: Autism Spectrum Disorder ISBN: 978-1-53612-730-0
Editors: R. Chow, J. Viehweger et al. ©2017 Nova Science Publishers, Inc.

Chapter 7

AWARENESS OF AUTISM SPECTRUM DISORDER AMONG YOUNG ADULTS IN WATERLOO, CANADA

Jaclyn Viehweger, BMSc(C), Ronald Chow*, BMSc(C) and Jerry Liu, BASc(C)
Infinitas Research Group, London, Ontario, Canada

Studies have looked into the awareness among young adults with respect to autism spectrum disorder (ASD). In this chapter we assess the awareness of young adults in Waterloo, Canada. A three-page survey was sent to young adults in Waterloo, Canada. Descriptive statistics were used to convey participant demographics, and also the responses provided by participants. Fisher exact tests were run to investigate whether different subgroups provided different responses. Subgroup analyses were conducted by age group (under/over 20 years old), sex (males/females), whether they have a family member with ASD, and whether they have a friend with ASD. P-values less than 0.05 were considered statistically significant. All statistical procedures were conducted using the Statistical Analysis Software. Of the 25 participants, 40% were between 20 and 22 years old, 32% were between 18 and 19 years old, 24% were over 22

* Correspondence: Ronald Chow BMSc(C), Infinitas Research Group, London, Ontario, Canada. Email: rchow48@uwo.ca.

years old, and 4% were under 18 years old. 84% were female, 32% knows of a family member affected by ASD, and 44% knows of a friend affected by ASD. 64% of young adults are knowledgeable about ASD. 32% and 44% of respondents know of a family member and friend, respectively, affected by ASD. These results as in-line with some prior studies. The subgroup analyses also indicated that there was no difference between demographic groups, which is also validating prior research.

INTRODUCTION

Studies (1-8) have looked into the awareness among young adults with respect to autism spectrum disorder (ASD), as it has been suggested that the awareness is indicative of the number of diagnosed cases of ASD (9,10). These studies have been carried out among young adults in London (1), Toronto (2), California (3), Montreal (4), Calgary (5), the United Kingdom (6), New York State (7) and Asia (8).

The results of the published literature (1-8) notes that the future prevalence of ASD may be approximately similar to current prevalence - however, future studies should investigate more rigorously this suggestion in longitudinal studies. Additionally, the data suggests that there is tremendous variation between the studies carried out in different geographical regions. The aim of our study was to assess the awareness of young adults in Waterloo, Canada.

OUR STUDY

A three-page survey was sent to young adults in Waterloo, Canada. The first page of three pages had a consent form listing the benefits/costs, and required participants to consent in order to complete the questionnaire. The second page collected participant demographics, and the third page assessed the perceived knowledge of ASD and also contained eight assessment questions (11).

Descriptive statistics were used to convey participant demographics, and also the responses provided by participants. Fisher exact tests were run to investigate whether different subgroups provided different responses. Subgroup analyses were conducted by age group (under/over 20 years old), sex (males/females), whether they have a family member with ASD, and whether they have a friend with ASD. P-values less than 0.05 were considered statistically significant. All statistical procedures were conducted using the Statistical Analysis Software (SAS Version 9.4 for Windows) (11).

FINDINGS

Of the 25 participants, 40% were between 20 and 22 years old, 32% were between 18 and 19 years old, 24% were over 22 years old, and 4% were under 18 years old. 84% were female, 32% knows of a family member affected by ASD, and 44% knows of a friend affected by ASD (see Table 1).

Table 1. Demographics

Demographic	**n = 25**
Age Group	
Under 18 years old	1 (4%)
18-19 years old	8 (32%)
20-22 years old	10 (40%)
Over 22 years old	6 (24%)
Sex	
Male	3 (12%)
Female	21 (84%)
Prefer not to say	1 (4%)
Family member affected by Autism	
Yes	8 (32%)
No	17 (68%)
Friend(s) affected by Autism	
Yes	11 (44%)
No	14 (56%)

Table 2. Perceived and actual knowledge

Question Item	n = 25
"I believe I am knowledgeable about Autism"	
Agree	12 (48%)
Disagree	0 (0%)
Neutral	13 (52%)
"Autism is a life-long developmental condition"	
True	22 (88%)
False	1 (4%)
Not Sure	2 (8%)
"Autism can be caused by poor parenting or parental behavior"	
True	0 (0%)
False	24 (96%)
Not Sure	1 (4%)
"The prevalence of Autism has increased over the years"	
True	17 (68%)
False	0 (0%)
Not Sure	8 (32%)
"Autism can arise from vaccinations"	
True	0 (0%)
False	24 (96%)
Not Sure	1 (4%)
"Individuals with Autism always prefer to be alone"	
True	1 (4%)
False	22 (88%)
Not Sure	2 (8%)
"People with Autism are eccentric geniuses"	
True	3 (12%)
False	20 (80%)
Not Sure	2 (8%)
"Individuals with Autism can grow out of it"	
True	3 (12%)
False	20 (80%)
Not Sure	2 (8%)
"People with Autism require substantial medical assistance"	
True	4 (16%)
False	13 (56%)
Not Sure	8 (32%)
Knowledge Score	
Not Knowledgeable (0-4)	2 (8%)
Satisfactory (5-6)	7 (28%)
Knowledgeable (7-8)	16 (64%)

48% of respondents believed they were aware of ASD. 88% and 96% correctly indicated that it is a life-long developmental condition, and that it cannot be a result of poor parenting. 68% and 96% noted that the prevalence has increased over the years and that it does not arise from vaccinations. 88%, 80%, 80% and 56%, respectively, indicated that individuals do not prefer to be alone, they are not all eccentric geniuses, individuals cannot grow out of it, and patients do not require substantial medical assistance. Overall, 64% were knowledgeable about ASD (see Table 2).

A larger proportion of those over 20 years old perceived themselves to be knowledgeable about ASD (p=0.0112) - 69% compared to 11% for those under 20 years old. There were no differences with respect to the individual assessment questions and the overall knowledge of the two cohorts. 100% and 81% remarked that it is a life-long developmental disorder (p=0.6870), and 100% and 94% noted that it cannot be caused by poor parenting (p=0.9999). 56% and 75% answered that the prevalence has increased over the years (p=0.3942), 89% and 100% indicated that it cannot arise from vaccinations (p=0.3600), and 100% and 81% reported that individuals do not always prefer to be alone (p=0.6870). 89% and 75% noted that they are not all eccentric geniuses (p=0.5874), 78% and 81% answered that individuals cannot grow out of it (p=0.4640) and 67% and 44% concluded that patients do not require substantial medical assistance (p=0.3846). Overall, 56% of those under 20 years old and 69% of those over 20 years old were knowledgeable about ASD (p=0.8354) (see Table 3).

Those who knew of a family member with ASD perceived themselves to be more knowledgeable (p=0.0112) - 88% compared to 29% believed they were knowledgeable. There were no difference in awareness level, however. 100% and 82% answered in the affirmative to the statement "Autism is a life-long developmental condition" (p=0.6846), and 88% and 59% to "the prevalence of Autism has increased over the years" (p=0.2052). 88% and 100% correctly rebuked the statement "Autism can be caused by poor parenting or parental behavior" (p=0.3200), 100% and 94% to "Autism can arise from vaccinations" (p=0.9999), 75% and 94% to

"Individuals with Autism always prefer to be alone" (p=0.2313), 75% and 82% to "People with Autism are eccentric geniuses" (p=0.9999), 75% and 82% to "Individuals with Autism can grow out of it" (p=0.9999) and 50% and 53% to "People with Autism require substantial medical assistance" (p=0.7186). Overall, 75% of those with a family member affected and 59% of those without one remarked were considered knowledgeable (p=0.4158). When comparing the responses of those with and without a friend affected by ASD, there was no difference in perceived awareness (p=0.4283) and actual knowledge (p=0.6946) (see Table 3).

Table 3. Perceived and actual knowledge - by subgroups

Question Item	**Under 20 n = 9**	**Over 20 n = 16**	**p-value**
"I believe I am knowledgeable about Autism"			0.0112
Agree	1 (11%)	11 (69%)	
Disagree	0 (0%)	0 (0%)	
Neutral	8 (89%)	5 (31%)	
"Autism is a life-long developmental condition"			0.6870
True	9 (100%)	13 (81%)	
False	0 (0%)	1 (6%)	
Not Sure	0 (0%)	2 (13%)	
"Autism can be caused by poor parenting or parental behavior"			0.9999
True	0 (0%)	0 (0%)	
False	9 (100%)	15 (94%)	
Not Sure	0 (0%)	1 (6%)	
"The prevalence of Autism has increased over the years"			0.3942
True	5 (56%)	12 (75%)	
False	0 (0%)	0 (0%)	
Not Sure	4 (45%)	4 (25%)	
"Autism can arise from vaccinations"			0.3600
True	0 (0%)	0 (0%)	
False	8 (89%)	16 (100%)	
Not Sure	1 (11%)	0 (0%)	

Question Item	**Under 20** **n = 9**	**Over 20** **n = 16**	**p-value**
"Individuals with Autism always prefer to be alone"			0.6870
True	0 (0%)	1 (6%)	
False	9 (100%)	13 (81%)	
Not Sure	0 (0%)	2 (13%)	
"People with Autism are eccentric geniuses"			0.5874
True	0 (0%)	3 (19%)	
False	8 (89%)	12 (75%)	
Not Sure	1 (11%)	1 (6%)	
"Individuals with Autism can grow out of it"			0.4640
True	2 (22%)	1 (6%)	
False	7 (78%)	13 (81%)	
Not Sure	0 (0%)	2 (13%)	
"People with Autism require substantial medical assistance"			0.3846
True	0 (0%)	4 (25%)	
False	6 (67%)	7 (44%)	
Not Sure	3 (33%)	5 (31%)	
Knowledge Score			0.8354
Not Knowledgeable (0-4)	1 (11%)	1 (6%)	
Satisfactory (5-6)	3 (33%)	4 (25%)	
Knowledgeable (7-8)	5 (56%)	11 (69%)	
Question Item	**Family affected** **n = 8**	**Family unaffected** **n = 17**	
"I believe I am knowledgeable about Autism"			0.0112
Agree	7 (88%)	5 (29%)	
Disagree	0 (0%)	0 (0%)	
Neutral	1 (13%)	12 (71%)	
"Autism is a life-long developmental condition"			0.6846
True	8 (100%)	14 (82%)	
False	0 (0%)	1 (6%)	
Not Sure	0 (0%)	2 (12%)	
"Autism can be caused by poor parenting or parental behavior"			0.3200
True	0 (0%)	0 (0%)	
False	7 (88%)	17 (100%)	
Not Sure	1 (13%)	0 (0%)	

Table 3. (Continued)

Question Item	Family affected n = 8	Family unaffected n = 17	
"The prevalence of Autism has increased over the years"			0.2052
True	7 (88%)	10 (59%)	
False	0 (0%)	0 (0%)	
Not Sure	1 (13%)	7 (41%)	
"Autism can arise from vaccinations"			0.9999
True	0 (0%)	0 (0%)	
False	8 (100%)	16 (94%)	
Not Sure	0 (0%)	1 (6%)	
"Individuals with Autism always prefer to be alone"			0.2313
True	1 (13%)	0 (0%)	
False	6 (75%)	16 (94%)	
Not Sure	1 (13%)	1 (6%)	
"People with Autism are eccentric geniuses"			0.9999
True	1 (13%)	2 (12%)	
False	6 (75%)	14 (82%)	
Not Sure	1 (13%)	1 (6%)	
"Individuals with Autism can grow out of it"			0.9999
True	1 (13%)	2 (12%)	
False	6 (75%)	14 (82%)	
Not Sure	1 (13%)	1 (6%)	
"People with Autism require substantial medical assistance"			0.7186
True	2 (25%)	2 (12%)	
False	4 (50%)	9 (53%)	
Not Sure	2 (25%)	6 (35%)	
Knowledge Score			0.4158
Not Knowledgeable (0-4)	1 (13%)	1 (6%)	
Satisfactory (5-6)	1 (13%)	6 (35%)	
Knowledgeable (7-8)	6 (75%)	10 (59%)	

Question Item	**Friend affected n = 11**	**Friend unaffected n = 14**	
"I believe I am knowledgeable about Autism"			0.4283
Agree	4 (45%)	8 (57%)	
Disagree	0 (0%)	0 (0%)	
Neutral	7 (64%)	6 (43%)	
"Autism is a life-long developmental condition"			0.3284
True	10 (91%)	12 (86%)	
False	1 (9%)	0 (0%)	
Not Sure	0 (0%)	2 (14%)	
"Autism can be caused by poor parenting or parental behavior"			0.4400
True	0 (0%)	0 (0%)	
False	10 (91%)	14 (100%)	
Not Sure	1 (9%)	0 (0%)	
"The prevalence of Autism has increased over the years"			0.9999
True	8 (73%)	9 (64%)	
False	0 (0%)	0 (0%)	
Not Sure	3 (27%)	5 (36%)	
"Autism can arise from vaccinations"			0.9999
True	0 (0%)	0 (0%)	
False	11 (100%)	13 (93%)	
Not Sure	0 (0%)	1 (7%)	
"Individuals with Autism always prefer to be alone"			0.7099
True	1 (9%)	0 (0%)	
False	9 (82%)	13 (93%)	
Not Sure	1 (9%)	1 (7%)	
"People with Autism are eccentric geniuses"			0.7739
True	2 (18%)	1 (7%)	
False	8 (73%)	12 (86%)	
Not Sure	1 (9%)	1 (7%)	
"Individuals with Autism can grow out of it"			0.4800
True	2 (18%)	1 (7%)	
False	9 (82%)	11 (79%)	
Not Sure	0 (0%)	2 (14%)	

Table 3. (Continued)

Question Item	Friend affected n = 11	Friend unaffected n = 14	
"People with Autism require substantial medical assistance"			0.6416
True	1 (9%)	3 (21%)	
False	7 (64%)	6 (43%)	
Not Sure	3 (27%)	5 (36%)	
Knowledge Score			0.6946
Not Knowledgeable (0-4)	1 (9%)	1 (7%)	
Satisfactory (5-6)	2 (18%)	5 (36%)	
Knowledgeable (7-8)	8 (73%)	8 (57%)	

DISCUSSION

The results of this study reveals that 64% of young adults in Waterloo are knowledgeable about ASD. A greater proportion are aware than the proportion of those who know of a family member (32%) of a friend (44%), which may suggest that future number of diagnosed cases may be slightly higher if not the same as today. These results are in line with a prior study looking into young adults in London, Canada (1).

Subgroup analyses suggested that those who are older and also those who know of an affected family member perceived themselves to be more knowledgeable. However, in line with other studies (1-8), there is actually no difference in actual awareness.

This study was not without limitations. As it is a survey study, there exists the possibility of a survey or response bias.

In conclusion, 64% of young adults are knowledgeable about ASD. 32% and 44% of respondents know of a family member and friend, respectively, affected by ASD. These results as in-line with some prior studies. The subgroup analyses also indicated that there was no difference between demographic groups, which is also validating prior research.

REFERENCES

[1] Chow R, Viehweger J, Anpalagan T, Yang H, Banerjee R. Awareness of autism spectrum disorder among young adults in London, Canada. Int Public Health J 2019;11(1), in press.

[2] Chow R, Viehweger J, Hollenberg D, Ho C, Ng W, Wong M. Awareness of autism spectrum disorder among young adults in Toronto, Canada. Int Public Health J 2019;11(1), in press.

[3] Chow R, Viehweger J, Murai A. Awareness of autism spectrum disorder among young adults in California, USA. Int Public Health J 2019;11(1), in press.

[4] Viehweger J, Chow R, Borean M. Awareness of autism spectrum disorder among young adults in Montreal, Canada. Int Public Health J 2019;11(1), in press.

[5] Chow R, Viehweger J. Awareness of autism spectrum disorder among young adults in Calgary, Canada. Int Public Health J 2019;11(1), in press.

[6] Viehweger J, Chow R, Goh S. Awareness of autism spectrum disorder among young adults in United Kingdom. Int Public Health J 2019;11(1), in press.

[7] Viehweger J, Chow R, Ganguli N. Awareness of autism spectrum disorder among young adults in New York State, USA. Int Public Health J 2019;11(1), in press.

[8] Viehweger J, Chow R. Awareness of autism spectrum disorder among young adults in Asia. Int Public Health J 2019;11(1), in press.

[9] Fombonne E, Zakarian R, Bennett A, Meng L, McLean-Heywood D. Pervasive developmental disorders in Montreal, Quebec, Canada: Prevalence and links with immunization. Pediatrics 2006;118:e139-50.

[10] Shattuck PT. The combination of diagnostic substitution to the growing administrative prevalence of autism in US special education data. Pediatrics 2006;117:1028-37.

[11] Chow R, Viehweger J. Assessing awareness of autism spectrum disorder: about the survey instrument. Int Public Health J 2019;11(1), in press.

In: Autism Spectrum Disorder ISBN: 978-1-53612-730-0
Editors: R. Chow, J. Viehweger et al. ©2017 Nova Science Publishers, Inc.

Chapter 8

AWARENESS OF AUTISM SPECTRUM DISORDER AMONG YOUNG ADULTS IN HAMILTON, CANADA

Drew Hollenberg, BMSc(C), Jaclyn Viehweger, BMSc(C) and Ronald Chow*, BMSc(C)
Infinitas Research Group, London, Ontario, Canada

Infinitas Research Group has investigated the awareness of autism symptom disorder (ASD) among young adults, who will be the future parents of society, in an attempt to indicate future prevalence. The results suggest that future prevalence may be approximately similar to current prevalence, but also revealed that there exists extreme variation between studies of different geographical regions. The aim of our study was to assess the awareness of young adults in Hamilton, Canada. 22 respondents consented and complete the survey - 64% were between 18 and 19 years old, 77% were female, 23% knew of a family member affected by ASD and 45% knew of a friend affected by ASD. 36% were knowledgeable about ASD, which is an intermediate statistic to the 23% who have a family member affected and 45% who have a friend affected.

* Correspondence: Ronald Chow BMSc(C), Infinitas Research Group, London, Ontario, Canada. Email: rchow48@uwo.ca.

This suggests that future prevalence may be approximately equal to current prevalence, as the percentage of those aware are not significantly greater than the percentage of those who knew of a friend with ASD. Longitudinal studies should look into whether this conclusion withstands the test of time. Subgroup analyses indicated that neither age, sex, or ties to ASD individuals increases the awareness of ASD. Future studies should look into discovering factors that increase awareness, as it seems that familial ties and ties to affected friends.

INTRODUCTION

Studying the awareness of autism spectrum disorder (ASD) may allow for the indication for future prevalence of ASD, as it has been suggested that prevalence is correlated with the awareness of ASD among parents (1-2).

Infinitas Research Group has investigated the awareness of ASD among young adults, who will be the future parents of society, in an attempt to indicate future prevalence. These studies have been conducted in London (3), Toronto (4), California (5), Montreal (6), Calgary (7), the United Kingdom (8), New York State (9), Asia (10) and Waterloo (11). The results suggest that future prevalence may be approximately similar to current prevalence, but also revealed that there exists extreme variation between studies of different geographical regions. The aim of our study was to assess the awareness of young adults in Hamilton, Canada.

THE SURVEY

A questionnaire was sent to young adults in Hamilton, Canada. The first page of three pages had a consent form listing the benefits/costs, and required participants to consent in order to complete the questionnaire. The second page collected participant demographics, and the third page assessed the perceived knowledge of ASD and also contained eight assessment questions (12).

Table 1. Demographics

Demographic	n = 22
Age Group	
Under 18 years old	2 (9%)
18-19 years old	14 (64%)
20-22 years old	4 (18%)
Over 22 years old	2 (9%)
Sex	
Male	4 (18%)
Female	17 (77%)
Prefer not to say	1 (5%)
Family member affected by Autism	
Yes	5 (23%)
No	17 (77%)
Friend(s) affected by Autism	
Yes	10 (45%)
No	12 (55%)

Descriptive statistics were used to convey participant demographics, and also the responses provided by participants. Fisher exact tests were run to investigate whether different subgroups provided different responses. Subgroup analyses were conducted by age group (under/over 20 years old), sex (males/females), whether they have a family member with ASD, and whether they have a friend with ASD. P-values less than 0.05 were considered statistically significant. All statistical procedures were conducted using the Statistical Analysis Software (SAS Version 9.4 for Windows) (12).

FINDINGS

22 respondents consented and completed the survey, 64% were between 18 and 19 years old, 77% were female, 23% knew of a family member affected by ASD and 45% knew of a friend affected by ASD (see Table 1).

Table 2. Perceived and actual knowledge

Question Item	n = 22
"I believe I am knowledgeable about Autism"	
Agree	8 (36%)
Disagree	5 (23%)
Neutral	9 (41%)
"Autism is a life-long developmental condition"	
True	19 (86%)
False	1 (5%)
Not Sure	2 (9%)
"Autism can be caused by poor parenting or parental behavior"	
True	0 (0%)
False	20 (91%)
Not Sure	2 (9%)
"The prevalence of Autism has increased over the years"	
True	10 (45%)
False	5 (23%)
Not Sure	7 (32%)
"Autism can arise from vaccinations"	
True	0 (0%)
False	20 (91%)
Not Sure	2 (9%)
"Individuals with Autism always prefer to be alone"	
True	0 (0%)
False	20 (91%)
Not Sure	2 (9%)
"People with Autism are eccentric geniuses"	
True	1 (5%)
False	17 (77%)
Not Sure	4 (18%)
"Individuals with Autism can grow out of it"	
True	0 (0%)
False	15 (68%)
Not Sure	7 (32%)
"People with Autism require substantial medical assistance"	
True	2 (9%)
False	12 (55%)
Not Sure	8 (36%)
Knowledge Score	
Not Knowledgeable (0-4)	1 (5%)
Satisfactory (5-6)	13 (59%)
Knowledgeable (7-8)	8 (36%)

36% of participants perceived themselves to be knowledgeable about ASD. 86% and 45% answered in the affirmative to the statements "Autism is a lifelong developmental condition" and "the prevalence of autism has increased over the years". 91%, 91% and 91% indicated that it cannot be caused by poor parenting, it cannot arise from vaccinations, and individuals do not always prefer to be alone, respectively. 77%, 68% and 55% responded that not all affected people are eccentric geniuses, individuals do not grow out of it, and they do not require substantial medical assistance. 36% were knowledgeable about ASD (see Table 2).

Those who knew of a family member affected by ASD believed they were more knowledgeable about ASD ($p = 0.0341$). There was no difference in actual awareness between the two cohorts ($p = 0.9999$). There were no other differences in perceived and actual awareness between the ages, sex, and those with and without friends affected by ASD (see Table 3).

Table 3. Perceived and actual knowledge - by subgroups

Question Item	**Under 20 n = 16**	**Over 20 n = 6**	**p-value**
"I believe I am knowledgeable about Autism"			0.2840
Agree	6 (38%)	2 (33%)	
Disagree	5 (31%)	0 (0%)	
Neutral	5 (31%)	4 (67%)	
"Autism is a life-long developmental condition"			0.9999
True	13 (81%)	6 (100%)	
False	1 (6%)	0 (0%)	
Not Sure	2 (13%)	0 (0%)	
"Autism can be caused by poor parenting or parental behavior"			0.9999
True	0 (0%)	0 (0%)	
False	14 (88%)	6 (100%)	
Not Sure	2 (13%)	0 (0%)	
"The prevalence of Autism has increased over the years"			0.9999
True	7 (44%)	3 (50%)	
False	4 (25%)	1 (17%)	
Not Sure	5 (31%)	2 (33%)	

Table 3. (Continued)

Question Item	**Under 20** **n = 16**	**Over 20** **n = 6**	**p-value**
"Autism can arise from vaccinations"			0.9999
True	0 (0%)	0 (0%)	
False	14 (88%)	6 (100%)	
Not Sure	2 (13%)	0 (0%)	
"Individuals with Autism always prefer to be alone"			0.9999
True	0 (0%)	0 (0%)	
False	14 (88%)	6 (100%)	
Not Sure	2 (13%)	0 (0%)	
"People with Autism are eccentric geniuses"			0.4769
True	1 (6%)	0 (0%)	
False	11 (69%)	6 (100%)	
Not Sure	4 (25%)	0 (0%)	
"Individuals with Autism can grow out of it"			0.9999
True	0 (0%)	0 (0%)	
False	11 (69%)	4 (67%)	
Not Sure	5 (31%)	2 (33%)	
"People with Autism require substantial medical assistance"			0.8142
True	2 (13%)	0 (0%)	
False	9 (56%)	3 (50%)	
Not Sure	5 (31%)	3 (50%)	
Knowledge Score			0.7317
Not Knowledgeable (0-4)	1 (6%)	0 (0%)	
Satisfactory (5-6)	10 (63%)	3 (50%)	
Knowledgeable (7-8)	5 (31%)	3 (50%)	
Question Item	**Males** **n = 4**	**Females** **n = 17**	
"I believe I am knowledgeable about Autism"			0.9999
Agree	1 (25%)	6 (35%)	
Disagree	1 (25%)	4 (24%)	
Neutral	2 (50%)	7 (41%)	
"Autism is a life-long developmental condition"			0.0797
True			
False	2 (50%)	16 (94%)	
Not Sure	1 (25%)	0 (0%)	
	1 (25%)	1 (6%)	

Question Item	**Males n = 4**	**Females n = 17**	
"Autism can be caused by poor parenting or parental behavior"			0.3524
True	0 (0%)	0 (0%)	
False	3 (75%)	16 (84%)	
Not Sure	1 (25%)	1 (6%)	
"The prevalence of Autism has increased over the years"			0.3509
True	3 (75%)	7 (41%)	
False	1 (25%)	3 (18%)	
Not Sure	0 (0%)	7 (41%)	
"Autism can arise from vaccinations"			0.9999
True	0 (0%)	0 (0%)	
False	4 (100%)	15 (88%)	
Not Sure	0 (0%)	2 (12%)	
"Individuals with Autism always prefer to be alone"			0.3524
True	0 (0%)	0 (0%)	
False	3 (75%)	16 (94%)	
Not Sure	1 (25%)	1 (6%)	
"People with Autism are eccentric geniuses"			0.6257
True			
False	0 (0%)	1 (6%)	
Not Sure	4 (100%)	12 (71%)	
	0 (0%)	4 (24%)	
"Individuals with Autism can grow out of it"			0.0877
True	0 (0%)	0 (0%)	
False	1 (25%)	13 (76%)	
Not Sure	3 (75%)	4 (24%)	
"People with Autism require substantial medical assistance"			0.5221
True	1 (25%)	1 (6%)	
False	2 (50%)	9 (53%)	
Not Sure	1 (25%)	7 (41%)	
Knowledge Score			0.3918
Not Knowledgeable (0-4)	0 (0%)	1 (6%)	
Satisfactory (5-6)	4 (100%)	9 (53%)	
Knowledgeable (7-8)	0 (0%)	7 (41%)	

Table 3. (Continued)

Question Item	**Family affected n = 5**	**Family unaffected n = 17**	
"I believe I am knowledgeable about Autism"			0.0341
Agree	4 (80%)	4 (24%)	
Disagree	1 (20%)	4 (24%)	
Neutral	0 (0%)	9 (53%)	
"Autism is a life-long developmental condition"			0.2641
True	4 (80%)	15 (88%)	
False	1 (20%)	0 (0%)	
Not Sure	0 (0%)	2 (12%)	
"Autism can be caused by poor parenting or parental behavior"			0.9999
True	0 (0%)	0 (0%)	
False	5 (100%)	15 (88%)	
Not Sure	0 (0%)	2 (12%)	
"The prevalence of Autism has increased over the years"			0.9999
True	2 (40%)	8 (47%)	
False	1 (20%)	4 (24%)	
Not Sure	2 (40%)	5 (29%)	
"Autism can arise from vaccinations"			0.9999
True	0 (0%)	0 (0%)	
False	5 (100%)	15 (88%)	
Not Sure	0 (0%)	2 (12%)	
"Individuals with Autism always prefer to be alone"			0.9999
True	0 (0%)	0 (0%)	
False	5 (100%)	15 (88%)	
Not Sure	0 (0%)	2 (12%)	
"People with Autism are eccentric geniuses"			0.2486
True	1 (20%)	0 (0%)	
False	3 (60%)	14 (82%)	
Not Sure	1 (20%)	3 (18%)	
"Individuals with Autism can grow out of it"			0.9999
True	0 (0%)	0 (0%)	
False	4 (80%)	11 (65%)	
Not Sure	1 (20%)	6 (35%)	

Question Item	Family affected n = 5	Family unaffected n = 17	
"People with Autism require substantial medical assistance"			0.3350
True	1 (20%)	1 (6%)	
False	3 (60%)	9 (53%)	
Not Sure	1 (20%)	7 (41%)	
Knowledge Score			0.9999
Not Knowledgeable (0-4)	0 (0%)	1 (6%)	
Satisfactory (5-6)	3 (60%)	10 (59%)	
Knowledgeable (7-8)	2 (40%)	6 (35%)	
Question Item	**Friend affected n = 10**	**Friend unaffected n = 12**	
"I believe I am knowledgeable about Autism"			0.4817
Agree	4 (40%)	4 (33%)	
Disagree	1 (10%)	4 (33%)	
Neutral	5 (50%)	4 (33%)	
"Autism is a life-long developmental condition"			0.9999
True	9 (90%)	10 (83%)	
False	0 (0%)	1 (8%)	
Not Sure	1 (10%)	1 (8%)	
"Autism can be caused by poor parenting or parental behavior"			0.9999
True	0 (0%)	0 (0%)	
False	9 (90%)	11 (92%)	
Not Sure	1 (10%)	1 (8%)	
"The prevalence of Autism has increased over the years"			0.0414
True	3 (30%)	7 (58%)	
False	1 (10%)	4 (33%)	
Not Sure	6 (60%)	1 (8%)	
"Autism can arise from vaccinations"			0.1948
True	0 (0%)	0 (0%)	
False	8 (80%)	12 (100%)	
Not Sure	2 (20%)	0 (0%)	
"Individuals with Autism always prefer to be alone"			0.4805
True	0 (0%)	0 (0%)	
False	10 (100%)	10 (83%)	
Not Sure	0 (0%)	2 (17%)	

Table 3. (Continued)

Question Item	Friend affected n = 10	Friend unaffected n = 12	
"People with Autism are eccentric geniuses"			0.2932
True	0 (0%)	1 (8%)	
False	7 (70%)	10 (83%)	
Not Sure	3 (30%)	1 (8%)	
"Individuals with Autism can grow out of it"			0.9999
True	0 (0%)	0 (0%)	
False	7 (70%)	8 (67%)	
Not Sure	3 (30%)	4 (33%)	
"People with Autism require substantial medical			0.9999
assistance"	1 (10%)	1 (8%)	
True	5 (50%)	7 (58%)	
False	4 (40%)	4 (33%)	
Not Sure			
Knowledge Score			0.1300
Not Knowledgeable (0-4)	0 (0%)	1 (8%)	
Satisfactory (5-6)	8 (80%)	5 (42%)	
Knowledgeable (7-8)	2 (20%)	6 (50%)	

DISCUSSION

The results of this study indicate that young adults in Hamilton are more knowledgeable than they need to be, to simply understand the condition their family members undergo - 36% were knowledgeable, compared to 23% of individuals having family member affected. The percentage of individuals who were aware of ASD was less than the percentage of those with a friend affected (45%). When interpreted together, this suggests that future prevalence may be approximately equal to current prevalence, as the percentage of those aware are not significantly greater than the percentage of those who knew of a friend with ASD. Longitudinal studies should look into whether this conclusion holds the test of time.

Subgroup analyses indicated that neither age, sex, or ties to ASD individuals increases the awareness of ASD. Future studies should look into discovering factors that increase awareness, as it seems that familial ties and ties to affected friends.

This study was not without limitations. As it is a survey study, there exists the possibility of a response and sampling bias. As the sample size was not too large, we examined the individual responses to try to identify any anomalies.

In conclusion, 36% were knowledgeable about ASD, which is an intermediate statistic to the 23% who have a family member affected and 45% who have a friend affected. This suggests that future prevalence may be approximately equal to current prevalence, as the percentage of those aware are not significantly greater than the percentage of those who knew of a friend with ASD. Longitudinal studies should look into whether this conclusion holds the test of time.

ACKNOWLEDGMENTS

We would like to thank Michael Borean, Tharani Anpalagan and Victoria Trasente for their support.

REFERENCES

[1] Fombonne E, Zakarian R, Bennett A, Meng L, McLean-Heywood D. Pervasive developmental disorders in Montreal, Quebec, Canada: Prevalence and links with immunization. Pediatrics 2006;118:e139-50.

[2] Shattuck PT. The combination of diagnostic substitution to the growing administrative prevalence of autism in US special education data. Pediatrics 2006;117:1028-37.

[3] Chow R, Viehweger J, Anpalagan T, Yang H, Banerjee R. Awareness of autism spectrum disorder among young adults in London, Canada. Int Public Health J 2019;11(1), in press.

[4] Chow R, Viehweger J, Hollenberg D, Ho C, Ng W, Wong M. Awareness of autism spectrum disorder among young adults in Toronto, Canada. Int Public Health J 2019;11(1), in press.

[5] Chow R, Viehweger J, Murai A. Awareness of autism spectrum disorder among young adults in California, USA. Int Public Health J 2019;11(1), in press.

[6] Viehweger J, Chow R, Borean M. Awareness of autism spectrum disorder among young adults in Montreal, Canada. Int Public Health J 2019;11(1), in press.

[7] Chow R, Viehweger J. Awareness of autism spectrum disorder among young adults in Calgary, Canada. Int Public Health J 2019;11(1), in press.

[8] Viehweger J, Chow R, Goh S. Awareness of autism spectrum disorder among young adults in United Kingdom. Int Public Health J 2019;11(1), in press.

[9] Viehweger J, Chow R, Ganguli N. Awareness of autism spectrum disorder among young adults in New York State, USA. Int Public Health J 2019;11(1), in press.

[10] Viehweger J, Chow R. Awareness of autism spectrum disorder among young adults in Asia. Int Public Health J 2019;11(1), in press.

[11] Viehweger J, Chow R, Liu J. Awareness of autism spectrum disorder among young adults in Waterloo, Canada. Int Public Health J 2019;11(1), in press.

[12] Chow R, Viehweger J. Assessing awareness of autism spectrum disorder: about the survey instrument. Int Public Health J 2019;11(1), in press.

SECTION TWO: UNITED STATES, UNITED KINGDOM AND ASIA

In: Autism Spectrum Disorder ISBN: 978-1-53612-730-0
Editors: R. Chow, J. Viehweger et al. ©2017 Nova Science Publishers, Inc.

Chapter 9

AWARENESS OF AUTISM SPECTRUM DISORDER AMONG YOUNG ADULTS IN NEW YORK STATE, USA

Jaclyn Viehweger, BMSc(C), Ronald Chow*, BMSc(C) and Neal Ganguli, BSc(C)
Infinitas Research Group, London, Ontario, Canada

Survey studies have been conducted to assess the awareness of young adults with respect to autism spectrum disorder. The studies have suggested that future prevalence may be similar to current prevalence, as a result of surveying young adults in London (Canada), Toronto, California, Montreal, Calgary and the United Kingdom. Across the studies, however, there exists tremendous variation in the awareness rate. The aim of this study was to assess the awareness of young adults in New York State, United States of America. A multi-page questionnaire was sent to young adults via social media. The majority (46%) of the 24 individuals who completed the survey were between 18 and 19 years old. 71% remarked they were female, 42% had a family member affected by ASD (to their knowledge), and 58% had a friend affected by ASD. Our results reveal that 58% were aware of ASD. 42% had a family member

* Correspondence: Ronald Chow BMSc(C), Infinitas Research Group, London, Ontario, Canada. Email: rchow48@uwo.ca.

and 58% had a friend affected by ASD; interpreting these statistics together seems to suggest that future prevalence may be similar to today's prevalence, but longitudinal studies should more rigorously investigate this research question.

Introduction

Survey studies have been conducted by Infinitas Research Group to assess the awareness of young adults with respect to autism spectrum disorder (ASD). The aim of these surveys have been to record the awareness of ASD and hopefully extrapolate from the data future prevalence of the disease, as previous literature has suggested that there exists a positive correlation between awareness (among parents) and diagnosed cases of ASD (1, 2).

The studies have suggested that future prevalence may be similar to current prevalence, as a result of surveying young adults in London (Canada) (3), Toronto (4), California (5), Montreal (6), Calgary (7) and the United Kingdom (8). Across the studies, however, there exists tremendous variation in the awareness rate. The aim of this study was to assess the awareness of young adults in New York State, United States of America.

Our Questionnaire

A multi-page questionnaire was sent to young adults in New York State, United States of America, via social media. The first page had a consent form listing the benefits/costs, and required participants to consent in order to complete the questionnaire. The second page collected participant demographics, and the third page assessed the perceived knowledge of ASD and also contained eight assessment questions (9).

Descriptive statistics were used to convey participant demographics, and also the responses provided by participants. Fisher exact tests were run to investigate whether different subgroups provided different responses. Subgroup analyses were conducted by age group (under/over 20 years old), sex (males/females), whether they have a family member with ASD, and whether they have a friend with ASD. P-values less than 0.05 were considered statistically significant. All statistical procedures were conducted using the Statistical Analysis Software (SAS Version 9.4 for Windows) (9).

FINDINGS

The majority (46%) of the 24 individuals who completed the survey were between 18 and 19 years old. 71% remarked they were female, 42% had a family member affected by ASD (to their knowledge), and 58% had a friend affected by ASD (see Table 1).

Table 1. Demographics

Demographic	**n = 24**
Age Group	
Under 18 years old	6 (25%)
18-19 years old	11 (46%)
20-22 years old	5 (21%)
Over 22 years old	2 (8%)
Sex	
Male	6 (25%)
Female	17 (71%)
Prefer not to say	1 (4%)
Family member affected by Autism	
Yes	10 (42%)
No	14 (58%)
Friend(s) affected by Autism	
Yes	14 (58%)
No	10 (42%)

Table 2. Perceived and actual knowledge

Question Item	n = 24
"I believe I am knowledgeable about Autism"	
Agree	15 (63%)
Disagree	2 (8%)
Neutral	7 (29%)
"Autism is a life-long developmental condition"	
True	21 (88%)
False	2 (8%)
Not Sure	1 (4%)
"Autism can be caused by poor parenting or parental behavior"	
True	0 (0%)
False	24 (100%)
Not Sure	0 (0%)
"The prevalence of Autism has increased over the years"	
True	18 (75%)
False	1 (4%)
Not Sure	5 (21%)
"Autism can arise from vaccinations"	
True	1 (4%)
False	21 (88%)
Not Sure	2 (8%)
"Individuals with Autism always prefer to be alone"	
True	0 (0%)
False	22 (92%)
Not Sure	2 (8%)
"People with Autism are eccentric geniuses"	
True	1 (4%)
False	19 (79%)
Not Sure	4 (17%)
"Individuals with Autism can grow out of it"	
True	3 (13%)
False	18 (75%)
Not Sure	3 (13%)
"People with Autism require substantial medical assistance"	
True	6 (25%)
False	11 (46%)
Not Sure	7 (29%)
Knowledge Score	
Not Knowledgeable (0-4)	2 (8%)
Satisfactory (5-6)	8 (33%)
Knowledgeable (7-8)	14 (58%)

63% of respondents believed they were knowledgeable about ASD. 88% and 75% responded that it is a lifelong developmental condition, and that the prevalence has increased over the years. 100% indicated that it is not caused by poor parenting, 88% noted that it cannot arise from vaccinations, 92% remarked that individuals do not always prefer to be alone, 79% concluded that not all are eccentric geniuses, 75% recorded that people do not grow out of ASD, and 46% concluded that patients do not require substantial medical assistance. Overall, 58% of young adults were aware of ASD (see Table 2).

When analyzing the responses by age, there was no difference in perceived and actual awareness between those over and under 20 years old. 59% and 71% of the groups, respectively, believed they were knowledgeable about ASD (p=0.9999). 88% and 86% answered that it is a lifelong developmental condition (p=0.6640); 100% and 100% that it is not caused by poor parenting (p=0.9999); 71% and 86% that is prevalence has increased over the years (p=0.9999); 82% and 100% that it cannot arise from vaccinations (p=0.9999); 88% and 100% that individuals do not prefer to be alone (p=0.9999); 71% and 100% that not all are eccentric geniuses (p=0.4848); 71% and 86% that individuals can grow out of it (p=0.7772); 47% and 43% that patients require substantial medical assistance (p=0.9999). Overall, 47% and 86% were knowledgeable about ASD (p=0.2302) (see Table 3).

There was no difference in perceived (p=0.7918) and actual (p=0.9999) knowledge between males and females. Males and females, respectively, answered affirmative to the statement "Autism is a lifelong developmental condition" at a frequency of 83% and 88% (p=0.6160), and to "the prevalence of autism has increased over the years" at 83% and 71% (p=0.9999). The two sexes answered "False" to the statements of "Autism can be caused by poor parenting or parental behavior" at 100% and 100% (p=0.9999), "Autism can arise from vaccinations" at 100% and 82% (p=0.9999), "Individuals with autism always prefer to be alone" at 100% and 88% (p=0.9999), "People with autism are eccentric geniuses" at 100% and 71% (p=0.6605), "Individuals with autism can grow out of it" at 83%

and 71% (p=0.7878), and "People with autism require substantial medical assistance" at 33% and 53% (p=0.4655) (see Table 3).

When comparing the responses of those with and without family members affected by ASD, there was no difference in perceptual (p=0.3722) and actual (p=0.2109) awareness. Similarly, there were no differences (p=0.4615, and p=0.8285) between those respondents who knew of and did not know of a friend with ASD (see Table 3).

Table 3. Perceived and actual knowledge - by subgroups

Question Item	Under 20 n = 17	Over 20 n = 7	p-value
"I believe I am knowledgeable about Autism"			0.9999
Agree	10 (59%)	5 (71%)	
Disagree	2 (12%)	0 (0%)	
Neutral	5 (29%)	2 (29%)	
"Autism is a life-long developmental condition"			0.6640
True	15 (88%)	6 (86%)	
False	1 (6%)	1 (14%)	
Not Sure	1 (6%)	0 (0%)	
"Autism can be caused by poor parenting or parental behavior"			0.9999
True	0 (0%)	0 (0%)	
False	17 (100%)	7 (100%)	
Not Sure	0 (0%)	0 (0%)	
"The prevalence of Autism has increased over the years"			0.9999
True	12 (71%)	6 (86%)	
False	1 (6%)	0 (0%)	
Not Sure	4 (24%)	1 (14%)	
"Autism can arise from vaccinations"			0.9999
True	1 (6%)	0 (0%)	
False	14 (82%)	7 (100%)	
Not Sure	2 (12%)	0 (0%)	

Question Item	**Under 20 n = 17**	**Over 20 n = 7**	**p-value**
"Individuals with Autism always prefer to be alone"			0.9999
True	0 (0%)	0 (0%)	
False	15 (88%)	7 (100%)	
Not Sure	2 (12%)	0 (0%)	
"People with Autism are eccentric geniuses"			0.4848
True	1 (6%)	0 (0%)	
False	12 (71%)	7 (100%)	
Not Sure	4 (23%)	0 (0%)	
"Individuals with Autism can grow out of it"			0.7772
True	2 (12%)	1 (14%)	
False	12 (71%)	6 (86%)	
Not Sure	3 (18%)	0 (0%)	
"People with Autism require substantial medical assistance"			0.9999
True	4 (24%)	2 (29%)	
False	8 (47%)	3 (43%)	
Not Sure	5 (29%)	2 (29%)	
Knowledge Score			0.2302
Not Knowledgeable (0-4)	2 (12%)	0 (0%)	
Satisfactory (5-6)	7 (41%)	1 (14%)	
Knowledgeable (7-8)	8 (47%)	6 (86%)	
Question Item	**Males n = 6**	**Females n = 17**	
"I believe I am knowledgeable about Autism"			0.7918
Agree	3 (50%)	11 (65%)	
Disagree	1 (17%)	1 (6%)	
Neutral	2 (33%)	5 (29%)	
"Autism is a life-long developmental condition"			0.6160
True	5 (83%)	15 (88%)	
False	1 (17%)	1 (6%)	
Not Sure	0 (0%)	1 (6%)	
"Autism can be caused by poor parenting or parental behavior"			0.9999
True	0 (0%)	0 (0%)	
False	6 (100%)	17 (100%)	
Not Sure	0 (0%)	0 (0%)	

Table 3. (Continued)

Question Item	**Males n = 6**	**Females n = 17**	
"The prevalence of Autism has increased over the years"			0.9999
True	5 (83%)	12 (71%)	
False	0 (0%)	1 (6%)	
Not Sure	1 (17%)	4 (24%)	
"Autism can arise from vaccinations"			0.9999
True	0 (0%)	1 (6%)	
False	6 (100%)	14 (82%)	
Not Sure	0 (0%)	2 (12%)	
"Individuals with Autism always prefer to be alone"			0.9999
True	0 (0%)	0 (0%)	
False	6 (100%)	15 (88%)	
Not Sure	0 (0%)	2 (12%)	
"People with Autism are eccentric geniuses"			0.6605
True	0 (0%)	1 (6%)	
False	6 (100%)	12 (71%)	
Not Sure	0 (0%)	4 (24%)	
"Individuals with Autism can grow out of it"			0.7878
True	0 (0%)	3 (18%)	
False	5 (83%)	12 (71%)	
Not Sure	1 (17%)	2 (12%)	
"People with Autism require substantial medical assistance"			0.4655
True	3 (50%)	3 (18%)	
False	2 (33%)	9 (53%)	
Not Sure	1 (17%)	5 (29%)	
Knowledge Score			0.9999
Not Knowledgeable (0-4)	0 (0%)	2 (12%)	
Satisfactory (5-6)	2 (33%)	6 (35%)	
Knowledgeable (7-8)	4 (67%)	9 (53%)	
Question Item	**Family affected n = 10**	**Family unaffected n = 14**	
"I believe I am knowledgeable about Autism"			0.3722
Agree	8 (80%)	7 (50%)	
Disagree	0 (0%)	2 (14%)	
Neutral	2 (20%)	5 (36%)	

Question Item	**Family affected n = 10**	**Family unaffected n = 14**	
"Autism is a life-long developmental condition"			0.7003
True	8 (80%)	13 (93%)	
False	1 (10%)	1 (7%)	
Not Sure	1 (10%)	0 (0%)	
"Autism can be caused by poor parenting or parental behavior"			0.9999
True	0 (0%)	0 (0%)	
False	10 (100%)	14 (100%)	
Not Sure	0 (0%)	0 (0%)	
"The prevalence of Autism has increased over the years"			0.7769
True	7 (70%)	11 (79%)	
False	1 (10%)	0 (0%)	
Not Sure	2 (20%)	3 (21%)	
"Autism can arise from vaccinations"			0.9999
True	0 (0%)	1 (7%)	
False	9 (90%)	12 (86%)	
Not Sure	1 (10%)	1 (7%)	
"Individuals with Autism always prefer to be alone"			0.4928
True	0 (0%)	0 (0%)	
False	10 (100%)	12 (86%)	
Not Sure	0 (0%)	2 (14%)	
"People with Autism are eccentric geniuses"			0.7688
True	0 (0%)	1 (7%)	
False	9 (90%)	10 (71%)	
Not Sure	1 (10%)	3 (21%)	
"Individuals with Autism can grow out of it"			0.9999
True	1 (10%)	2 (14%)	
False	8 (80%)	10 (71%)	
Not Sure	1 (10%)	2 (14%)	
"People with Autism require substantial medical assistance"			0.0287
True	1 (10%)	5 (36%)	
False	8 (80%)	3 (21%)	
Not Sure	1 (10%)	6 (43%)	

Table 3. (Continued)

Question Item	**Family affected n = 10**	**Family unaffected n = 14**	
Knowledge Score			0.2109
Not Knowledgeable (0-4)	0 (0%)	2 (14%)	
Satisfactory (5-6)	2 (20%)	6 (43%)	
Knowledgeable (7-8)	8 (80%)	6 (43%)	
Question Item	**Friend affected n = 14**	**Friend unaffected n = 10**	
"I believe I am knowledgeable about Autism"			0.4615
Agree	9 (64%)	6 (60%)	
Disagree	2 (14%)	0 (0%)	
Neutral	3 (21%)	4 (40%)	
"Autism is a life-long developmental condition"			0.1630
True	13 (93%)	8 (80%)	
False	0 (0%)	2 (20%)	
Not Sure	1 (7%)	0 (0%)	
"Autism can be caused by poor parenting or parental behavior"			0.9999
True	0 (0%)	0 (0%)	
False	14 (100%)	10 (100%)	
Not Sure	0 (0%)	0 (0%)	
"The prevalence of Autism has increased over the years"			0.7769
True	11 (79%)	7 (70%)	
False	1 (7%)	0 (0%)	
Not Sure	2 (14%)	3 (30%)	
"Autism can arise from vaccinations"			0.3129
True	0 (0%)	1 (10%)	
False	12 (86%)	9 (90%)	
Not Sure	2 (14%)	0 (0%)	
"Individuals with Autism always prefer to be alone"			0.9999
True	0 (0%)	0 (0%)	
False	13 (93%)	9 (90%)	
Not Sure	1 (7%)	1 (10%)	

Question Item	**Friend affected n = 14**	**Friend unaffected n = 10**	
"People with Autism are eccentric geniuses"			0.5804
True	0 (0%)	1 (10%)	
False	11 (79%)	8 (80%)	
Not Sure	3 (21%)	1 (10%)	
"Individuals with Autism can grow out of it"			0.1393
True	0 (0%)	3 (30%)	
False	12 (86%)	6 (60%)	
Not Sure	2 (14%)	1 (10%)	
"People with Autism require substantial medical assistance"			0.8763
True	3 (21%)	3 (30%)	
False	7 (50%)	4 (40%)	
Not Sure	4 (29%)	3 (30%)	
Knowledge Score			0.8285
Not Knowledgeable (0-4)	1 (7%)	1 (10%)	
Satisfactory (5-6)	4 (29%)	4 (40%)	
Knowledgeable (7-8)	9 (64%)	5 (50%)	

DISCUSSION

Our study reveals that 58% of young adults were knowledgeable about ASD, which is on-par with the percentage of individuals with a friend affected by ASD (58%) and in excess of the proportion of respondents who have a family member affected by ASD (42%). This data seems to suggest that future prevalence may be similar to today's prevalence, however longitudinal studies should more rigorously investigate this suggestion.

There was no difference between the subgroups with respect to awareness, affirming previous conclusions from other literature (3-8). The suggestion regarding future prevalence is also in-line with previous studies (4-8).

This study was not without limitations. As it is a survey study, there exists the possibility of a sampling and response bias. In an attempt to mitigate this, we combed each response thoroughly before including in the analysis, just to quickly assess whether there were some anomalies (i.e., individuals who seem to purposely respond to all questions incorrectly) and removed them accordingly, if needed.

In conclusion, 58% were aware of ASD. 42% had a family member and 58% had a friend affected by ASD; interpreting these statistics together seems to suggest that future prevalence may be similar to today's prevalence, but longitudinal studies should more rigorously investigate this research question.

Acknowledgment

We would like to thank Tharani Anpalagan for the support.

References

[1] Fombonne E, Zakarian R, Bennett A, Meng L, McLean-Heywood D. Pervasive developmental disorders in Montreal, Quebec, Canada: Prevalence and links with immunization. Pediatrics 2006;118:e139-50.

[2] Shattuck PT. The combination of diagnostic substitution to the growing administrative prevalence of autism in US special education data. Pediatrics 2006;117:1028-37.

[3] Chow R, Viehweger J, Anpalagan T, Yang H, Banerjee R. Awareness of autism spectrum disorder among young adults in London, Canada. Int Public Health J 2019;11(1), in press.

[4] Chow R, Viehweger J, Hollenberg D, Ho C, Ng W, Wong M. Awareness of autism spectrum disorder among young adults in Toronto, Canada. Int Public Health J 2019;11(1), in press.

[5] Chow R, Viehweger J, Murai A. Awareness of autism spectrum disorder among young adults in California, USA. Int Public Health J 2019;11(1), in press.

[6] Viehweger J, Chow R, Borean M. Awareness of autism spectrum disorder among young adults in Montreal, Canada. Int Public Health J 2019;11(1), in press.

[7] Chow R, Viehweger J. Awareness of autism spectrum disorder among young adults in Calgary, Canada. Int Public Health J 2019;11(1), in press.

[8] Chow R, Viehweger J, Goh S. Awareness of autism spectrum disorder among young adults in United Kingdom. Int Public Health J 2019;11(1), in press.

[9] Chow R, Viehweger J. Assessing awareness of autism spectrum disorder: about the survey instrument. Int Public Health J 2019;11(1), in press.

In: Autism Spectrum Disorder ISBN: 978-1-53612-730-0
Editors: R. Chow, J. Viehweger et al. ©2017 Nova Science Publishers, Inc.

Chapter 10

AWARENESS OF AUTISM SPECTRUM DISORDER AMONG YOUNG ADULTS IN CALIFORNIA, USA

Ronald Chow*, BMSc(C),
Jaclyn Viehweger, BMSc(C)
and Adam Murai, BSc(C)
Infinitas Research Group, London, Ontario, Canada

Autism spectrum disorder (ASD) has been suggested to have an increased number of diagnosed cases over the past several decades as a result of greater awareness among parents. The aim of our study was to investigate the awareness of ASD in the American State of California. A three-page survey was sent to young adults in the American State of California. The first page had a consent form listing the benefits/costs, and required participants to consent in order to complete the questionnaire. The second page collected participant demographics, and the third page assessed the perceived knowledge of ASD and also contained eight assessment questions. Of the 28 young adults who completed the questionnaire, 50% were knowledgeable about the disorder - individuals are less aware than

* Correspondence: Ronald Chow BMSc(C), Infinitas Research Group, London, Ontario, Canada. Email: rchow48@uwo.ca.

they perceived themselves to be (61%). The statistics (50% with a family member affected by ASD, and 71% with a friend bearing ASD) shows that the awareness rate may be on par or slightly below the affected rate. Longitudinal studies should more rigorously investigate this trend to determine whether the future prevalence of ASD is approximately equal if not higher than today.

INTRODUCTION

Autism spectrum disorder (ASD) has been suggested to have an increased number of diagnosed cases over the past several decades as a result of greater awareness among parents (1, 2). Evaluating the awareness of ASD in today's young adults, and tomorrow's parents, may allow us to extrapolate the future prevalence of the ASD (3).

An original study by Chow et al. in London reported that 56% of young adults were aware of ASD. This statistic, when interpreted in lieu of the fact that 26% have a family member affected by ASD and 44% have a friend affected by ASD, suggests that awareness of ASD may be a result of not only exposure to afflicted individuals. The high awareness rate also suggests that future prevalence of ASD may increase (4).

A follow-up conducted in Toronto found slightly different results - variation in statistics and also a slightly different interpretation from the data. 26% had family member affected and 34% had a friend affected, which is similar to that reported in London that prevalence among friends is higher. 29% of young adults were aware of ASD; the observation that it is an intermediate value suggests that exposure to family, and not friends, may contribute a greater role to ASD awareness (5). The aim of our study was to further investigate the awareness of ASD.

THE SURVEY

A three-page survey was sent to young adults in the American State of California. The first page had a consent form listing the benefits/costs, and required participants to consent in order to complete the questionnaire. The second page collected participant demographics, and the third page assessed the perceived knowledge of ASD and also contained eight assessment questions (6).

Descriptive statistics were used to convey participant demographics, and also the responses provided by participants. Fisher exact tests were run to investigate whether different subgroups provided different responses. Subgroup analyses were conducted by age group (under/over 20 years old), sex (males/females), whether they have a family member with ASD, and whether they have a friend with ASD. P-values less than 0.05 were considered statistically significant. All statistical procedures were conducted using the Statistical Analysis Software (SAS Version 9.4 for Windows) (6).

OUR FINDINGS

28 young adults consented and completed the study. 15 (54%) were between 18 and 19 years old, 10 (36%) were between 20 and 22 years old, 2 (7%) were over 22 years old, and 1 (4%) were under 18 years old. 18 (64%) remarked that they were female, 9 (32%) identified themselves as male, and 1 (4%) did not identify their sex. 14 (50%) had a family member affected by ASD, and 20 (71%) had a friend affected by ASD (see Table 1).

Of the 28 participants, 17 (61%) perceived themselves as knowledgeable about the disorder. 93% and 64% remarked in the affirmative to the statements "Autism is a lifelong developmental condition" and "The prevalence of Autism has increased over the years", respectively. 86% noted that it is not a cause of poor parenting, 89%

indicated that it cannot arise from vaccinations, 93% answered that individuals do not always prefer to be alone, 82% concluded that they are not all eccentric geniuses, 68% remarked that individuals can not grow out of it, and 57% concluded that they do not require substantial medical assistance. 50% of participants were knowledgeable (see Table 2).

There was no difference in perceptual and actual awareness between the two age cohorts. 56% and 67% of those under and over 20 years old, respectively, believed they were knowledgeable ($p = 0.6021$). 38% and 67% of the same two groups were knowledgeable, based on the assessment questions ($p = 0.0825$). 88% and 100% noted that it is a lifelong developmental condition ($p = 0.4920$). 94% and 75% remarked that it is not a result of poor parenting ($p = 0.2850$). 56% and 75% remarked that the prevalence has increased over the years ($p = 0.6293$). 81% and 100% answered that it is not a result of vaccinations ($p = 0.2381$). 88% and 100% answered that individuals do not always prefer to be alone ($p = 0.9999$). 75% and 92% indicated that ASD individuals are not all eccentric geniuses ($p = 0.6132$). 63% and 75% noted that individuals cannot grow out of it ($p = 0.4286$). 56% and 58% marked that patients do not require substantial medical assistance ($p = 0.9999$) (see Table 3).

Table 1. Demographics

Demographic	n = 28
Age Group	
Under 18 years old	1 (4%)
18-19 years old	15 (54%)
20-22 years old	10 (36%)
Over 22 years old	2 (7%)
Sex	
Male	9 (32%)
Female	18 (64%)
Prefer not to say	1 (4%)
Family member affected by Autism	
Yes	14 (50%)
No	14 (50%)
Friend(s) affected by Autism	
Yes	20 (71%)
No	8 (29%)

Table 2. Perceived and actual knowledge

Question Item	n = 28
"I believe I am knowledgeable about Autism"	
Agree	17 (61%)
Disagree	2 (7%)
Neutral	9 (32%)
"Autism is a life-long developmental condition"	
True	26 (93%)
False	0 (0%)
Not Sure	2 (7%)
"Autism can be caused by poor parenting or parental behavior"	
True	0 (0%)
False	24 (86%)
Not Sure	4 (14%)
"The prevalence of Autism has increased over the ears"	
True	18 (64%)
False	3 (11%)
Not Sure	7 (25%)
"Autism can arise from vaccinations"	
True	0 (0%)
False	25 (89%)
Not Sure	3 (11%)
"Individuals with Autism always prefer to be alone"	
True	1 (4%)
False	26 (93%)
Not Sure	1 (4%)
"People with Autism are eccentric geniuses"	
True	2 (7%)
False	23 (82%)
Not Sure	3 (11%)
"Individuals with Autism can grow out of it"	
True	3 (11%)
False	19 (68%)
Not Sure	6 (21%)
"People with Autism require substantial medical assistance"	
True	6 (21%)
False	16 (57%)
Not Sure	6 (21%)
Knowledge Score	
Not Knowledgeable (0-4)	1 (4%)
Satisfactory (5-6)	13 (46%)
Knowledgeable (7-8)	14 (50%)

Table 3. Perceived and actual knowledge - by subgroups

Question Item	**Under 20** **n = 16**	**Over 20** **n = 12**	**p-value**
"I believe I am knowledgeable about Autism"			0.6021
Agree	9 (56%)	8 (67%)	
Disagree	2 (13%)	0 (0%)	
Neutral	5 (31%)	4 (33%)	
"Autism is a life-long developmental condition"			0.4920
True	14 (88%)	12 (100%)	
False	0 (0%)	0 (0%)	
Not Sure	2 (13%)	0 (0%)	
"Autism can be caused by poor parenting or parental behavior"			0.2850
True	0 (0%)	0 (0%)	
False	15 (94%)	9 (75%)	
Not Sure	1 (6%)	3 (25%)	
"The prevalence of Autism has increased over the years"			0.6293
True	9 (56%)	9 (75%)	
False	2 (13%)	1 (8%)	
Not Sure	5 (31%)	2 (17%)	
"Autism can arise from vaccinations"			0.2381
True	0 (0%)	0 (0%)	
False	13 (81%)	12 (100%)	
Not Sure	3 (19%)	0 (0%)	
"Individuals with Autism always prefer to be alone"			0.9999
True	1 (6%)	0 (0%)	
False	14 (88%)	12 (100%)	
Not Sure	1 (6%)	0 (0%)	
"People with Autism are eccentric geniuses"			0.6132
True	2 (13%)	0 (0%)	
False	12 (75%)	11 (92%)	
Not Sure	2 (13%)	1 (8%)	
"Individuals with Autism can grow out of it"			0.4286
True	3 (19%)	0 (0%)	
False	10 (63%)	9 (75%)	
Not Sure	3 (19%)	3 (25%)	
"People with Autism require substantial medical assistance"			0.9999
True	3 (19%)	3 (25%)	

Question Item	Under 20 n = 16	Over 20 n = 12	p-value
False	9 (56%)	7 (58%)	
Not Sure	4 (25%)	2 (17%)	
Knowledge Score			0.0825
Not Knowledgeable (0-4)	0 (0%)	1 (8%)	
Satisfactory (5-6)	10 (63%)	3 (25%)	
Knowledgeable (7-8)	6 (38%)	8 (67%)	
Question Item	**Males n = 9**	**Females n = 18**	
"I believe I am knowledgeable about Autism"			0.5769
Agree	5 (56%)	11 (61%)	
Disagree	0 (0%)	2 (11%)	
Neutral	4 (44%)	5 (28%)	
"Autism is a life-long developmental condition"			0.5385
True	9 (100%)	16 (89%)	
False	0 (0%)	0 (0%)	
Not Sure	0 (0%)	2 (11%)	
"Autism can be caused by poor parenting or parental behavior"			0.5815
True	0 (0%)	0 (0%)	
False	7 (78%)	16 (89%)	
Not Sure	2 (22%)	2 (11%)	
"The prevalence of Autism has increased over the years"			0.6026
True	7 (78%)	10 (56%)	
False	0 (0%)	3 (17%)	
Not Sure	2 (22%)	5 (28%)	
"Autism can arise from vaccinations"			0.9999
True	0 (0%)	0 (0%)	
False	8 (89%)	16 (89%)	
Not Sure	1 (11%)	2 (11%)	
"Individuals with Autism always prefer to be alone"			0.9999
True	0 (0%)	1 (6%)	
False	9 (100%)	16 (89%)	
Not Sure	0 (0%)	1 (6%)	
"People with Autism are eccentric geniuses"			0.7817
True	0 (0%)	2 (11%)	
False	8 (89%)	14 (78%)	
Not Sure	1 (11%)	2 (11%)	

Table 3. (Continued)

Question Item	**Males n = 9**	**Females n = 18**	
"Individuals with Autism can grow out of it"			0.5899
True	0 (0%)	3 (17%)	
False	7 (78%)	11 (61%)	
Not Sure	2 (22%)	4 (22%)	
"People with Autism require substantial medical assistance"			0.0881
True	1 (11%)	5 (28%)	
False	8 (89%)	8 (44%)	
Not Sure	0 (0%)	5 (28%)	
Knowledge Score			0.1317
Not Knowledgeable (0-4)	0 (0%)	1 (6%)	
Satisfactory (5-6)	2 (22%)	11 (61%)	
Knowledgeable (7-8)	7 (78%)	6 (33%)	
Question Item	**Family affected n = 14**	**Family unaffected n = 14**	
"I believe I am knowledgeable about Autism"			0.1032
Agree	11 (79%)	6 (43%)	
Disagree	1 (7%)	1 (7%)	
Neutral	2 (14%)	7 (50%)	
"Autism is a life-long developmental condition"			0.4815
True	14 (100%)	12 (86%)	
False	0 (0%)	0 (0%)	
Not Sure	0 (0%)	2 (14%)	
"Autism can be caused by poor parenting or parental behavior"			0.9999
True	0 (0%)	0 (0%)	
False	12 (86%)	12 (86%)	
Not Sure	2 (14%)	2 (14%)	
"The prevalence of Autism has increased over the years"			0.3790
True	7 (50%)	11 (79%)	
False	2 (14%)	1 (7%)	
Not Sure	5 (36%)	2 (14%)	
"Autism can arise from vaccinations"			0.6111
True	0 (0%)	0 (0%)	
False	13 (93%)	12 (86%)	
Not Sure	1 (7%)	2 (14%)	

Question Item	**Family affected n = 14**	**Family unaffected n = 14**	
"Individuals with Autism always prefer to be alone"			0.4815
True	1 (7%)	0 (0%)	
False	12 (86%)	14 (100%)	
Not Sure	1 (7%)	0 (0%)	
"People with Autism are eccentric geniuses"			0.1652
True	1 (7%)	1 (7%)	
False	13 (93%)	10 (71%)	
Not Sure	0 (0%)	3 (21%)	
"Individuals with Autism can grow out of it"			0.9999
True	2 (17%)	1 (7%)	
False	9 (64%)	10 (71%)	
Not Sure	3 (21%)	3 (21%)	
"People with Autism require substantial medical assistance"			0.9999
True	3 (21%)	3 (21%)	
False	8 (57%)	8 (57%)	
Not Sure	3 (21%)	3 (21%)	
Knowledge Score			0.9999
Not Knowledgeable (0-4)	1 (7%)	0 (0%)	
Satisfactory (5-6)	6 (43%)	7 (50%)	
Knowledgeable (7-8)	7 (50%)	7 (50%)	
Question Item	**Friend affected n = 20**	**Friend unaffected n = 8**	
"I believe I am knowledgeable about Autism"			0.1930
Agree	14 (70%)	3 (38%)	
Disagree	1 (5%)	1 (13%)	
Neutral	5 (25%)	4 (50%)	
"Autism is a life-long developmental condition"			0.9999
True	18 (90%)	8 (100%)	
False	0 (0%)	0 (0%)	
Not Sure	2 (10%)	0 (0%)	
"Autism can be caused by poor parenting or parental behavior"			0.5546
True	0 (0%)	0 (0%)	
False	18 (90%)	6 (75%)	
Not Sure	2 (10%)	2 (25%)	

Table 3. (Continued)

Question Item	Friend affected n = 20	Friend unaffected n = 8	
"The prevalence of Autism has increased over the years"			0.3039
True	14 (70%)	4 (50%)	
False	1 (5%)	2 (25%)	
Not Sure	5 (25%)	2 (25%)	
"Autism can arise from vaccinations"			0.5360
True	0 (0%)	0 (0%)	
False	17 (85%)	8 (100%)	
Not Sure	3 (15%)	0 (0%)	
"Individuals with Autism always prefer to be alone"			0.4974
True	1 (5%)	0 (0%)	
False	19 (95%)	7 (88%)	
Not Sure	0 (0%)	1 (13%)	
"People with Autism are eccentric geniuses"			0.2530
True	2 (10%)	0 (0%)	
False	17 (85%)	6 (75%)	
Not Sure	1 (5%)	2 (25%)	
"Individuals with Autism can grow out of it"			0.0013
True	2 (10%)	1 (13%)	
False	17 (85%)	2 (25%)	
Not Sure	1 (5%)	5 (63%)	
"People with Autism require substantial medical assistance"			0.9999
True	4 (20%)	2 (25%)	
False	12 (60%)	4 (50%)	
Not Sure	4 (20%)	2 (25%)	
Knowledge Score			0.5855
Not Knowledgeable (0-4)	1 (5%)	0 (0%)	
Satisfactory (5-6)	8 (40%)	5 (63%)	
Knowledgeable (7-8)	11 (55%)	3 (38%)	

Males and females were similar in the proportion of individuals who perceive themselves to be aware, and also who are actually aware of ASD. 56% and 61%, respectively, believed they were knowledgeable ($p = 0.5769$). 100% and 89% answered that ASD is a lifelong developmental condition ($p = 0.5385$); 78% and 89% that it is not a result of poor parenting ($p = 0.5815$); 78% and 56% that it has increased over the years ($p = 0.6026$); 89% of both that it is not a result of vaccinations ($p = 0.9999$); 100% and 89% that ASD individuals do not prefer to be alone ($p = 0.9999$); 89% and 78% that individuals are not all eccentric geniuses ($p = 0.7817$); 78% and 61% that individuals cannot grow out of it ($p = 0.5899$); 89% and 44% that individuals do not require substantial medical assistance ($p = 0.0881$). 78% and 33% of males and females, respectively, were knowledgeable ($p = 0.1317$) (see Table 3).

Among the subgroups of those with and without family members affected by ASD, there is no difference in perceptual and actual awareness. 79% and 43% of those with and without a family member affected, respectively, believed they were knowledgeable about ASD ($p = 0.1032$). 100% and 86% noted that it is a lifelong developmental disorder ($p = 0.4815$), 86% of both remarked that it is not caused by poor parenting ($p = 0.9999$), and 50% and 79% noted that its prevalence has increased over the years ($p = 0.3790$). 93% and 86% answered that it is not caused by vaccinations ($p = 0.6111$), 86% and 100% concluded that individuals do not always prefer to be alone ($p = 0.4815$), 93% and 71% indicated that ASD individuals are not eccentric geniuses ($p = 0.1652$), 64% and 71% remarked that individuals cannot grow out of it ($p = 0.9999$), and 57% and 71% noted that not all individuals require substantial medical assistance ($p = 0.9999$). 50% of both groups are knowledgeable about ASD ($p = 0.9999$) (see Table 3).

Perceived and actual awareness between groups with and without friends who are affected by ASD indicated that there was no difference. 70% and 38% of friends with and without an affected individuals, respectively, believe they were knowledgeable ($p = 0.193$). 90% and 100% correctly noted that ASD is a developmental condition ($p = 0.9999$), and 5% and 25% that the prevalence has increased over the years ($p = 0.3039$). 0% of both groups incorrectly responses that it is caused by poor parenting ($p = 0.5546$), 0% of both that it can be caused by vaccinations ($p = 0.5360$), 5% and 0% that individuals always prefer to be alone ($p = 0.4974$), 10% and 0% that not all affected individuals are eccentric geniuses ($p = 0.2530$), 10% and 13% that ASD patients can grow out of it ($p = 0.0013$), and 20% and 25% that ASD patients require substantial medical assistance ($p = 0.9999$). 55% and 38% were knowledgeable about ASD ($p = 0.5855$) (see Table 3).

DISCUSSION

The results reveal that 50% of respondents had a family member affected by ASD, and 71% had a friend affected by ASD. 50% were knowledgeable about the disorder, confirming a prior study that awareness may be a result of exposure to family members rather than to friends (5). The perceived awareness is greater than the actual awareness, which reports opposite findings (7-12).

When compared to other studies (4-5), a greater proportion of young adults surveyed in California knew of affected individuals. The awareness, consequently, seems to chart up slightly higher than other studies.

The statistics show that awareness rate may be on par or slightly below the affected rate. This may suggest that future prevalence of ASD may be approximately equal if not higher than today. Longitudinal studies should more rigorously investigate this trend.

This study was not without limitations. As this is a survey study, there exists the possibility of a sampling and response bias.

In conclusion, 50% were knowledgeable about the disorder - individuals are less aware than they perceived themselves to be (61%). The statistics (50% with a family member affected by ASD, and 71% with a friend bearing ASD) shows that the awareness rate may be on par or slightly below the affected rate. Longitudinal studies should more rigorously investigate this trend to determine whether the future prevalence of ASD is approximately equal if not higher than today.

ACKNOWLEDGMENT

We would like to thank Tharani Anpalagan for her support.

REFERENCES

[1] Fombonne E, Zakarian R, Bennett A, Meng L, McLean-Heywood D. Pervasive developmental disorders in Montreal, Quebec, Canada: prevalence and links with immunization. Pediatrics 2006;118:e139-50.

[2] Shattuck PT. The combination of diagnostic substitution to the growing administrative prevalence of autism in US special education data. Pediatrics 2006;117:1028-37.

[3] Chow R, Viehweger J. Are young adults aware of autism spectrum disorder? Int Public Health J 2019;11(1), in press.

[4] Chow R, Viehweger J, Anpalagan T, Yang H, Banerjee R. Awareness of autism spectrum disorder among young adults in London, Canada. Int Public Health J 2019;11(1), in press.

[5] Chow R, Viehweger J, Hollenberg D, Ho C, Ng W, Wong M. Awareness of autism spectrum disorder among young adults in Toronto, Canada. Int Public Health J 2019;11(1), in press.

[6] Chow R, Viehweger J. Assessing awareness of autism spectrum disorder: About the survey instrument. Int Public Health J 2019;11(1), in press.

[7] Chow R, Viehweger J, Trasente V, Borean M, Hollenberg D, Lam M, et al. Awareness of Parkinson's disease among young adults in London, Canada. J Pain Manage 2019;12(1), in press.

[8] Ho S, Viehweger J, Trasente V, Ho C, Ng W, Wong M, et al. Awareness of Parkinson's disease among young adults in Toronto, Canada. J Pain Manage 2019;12(1), in press.

[9] Viehweger J, Chow R, Trasente V, Duarte N, Borean M, Hollenberg D, et al. Awareness of Parkinson's disease among young adults in Waterloo, Canada. J Pain Manage 2019;12(1), in press.

[10] Chow R, Ferrara A, Borean M, Hollenberg D, Lam M, Anpalagan T, et al. Awareness of Alzheimer's disease among young adults in London, Canada. Int J Child Health Hum Dev 2018; in press.

[11] Chow R, Borean M, Hollenberg D, Midroni L, Midroni C, Kim Y, et al. Awareness of Alzheimer's disease among young adults in Kingston, Canada. Int J Child Health Hum Dev 2018; in press.

[12] Borean M, Rzepka A, Trasente V, Hollenberg D, Ho C, Ng W, et al. Awareness of Alzheimer's disease among young adults in Toronto, Canada. Int J Child Health Hum Dev 2018; in press.

In: Autism Spectrum Disorder ISBN: 978-1-53612-730-0
Editors: R. Chow, J. Viehweger et al. ©2017 Nova Science Publishers, Inc.

Chapter 11

AWARENESS OF AUTISM SPECTRUM DISORDER AMONG YOUNG ADULTS IN UNITED KINGDOM

Jaclyn Viehweger, BMSc(C), Ronald Chow*, BMSc(C) and Samuel Goh, MBChB(C)
Infinitas Research Group, London, Ontario, Canada

The awareness of young adults with respect to autism spectrum disorder (ASD) has been studied, as it has been suggested that the awareness of parents affects the number of diagnosed cases - there is a positive correlation between awareness and prevalence of ASD. There was tremendous variation between the studies, and no study has been performed yet to evaluate the awareness of young adults outside of North America. The aim of our study was to further look into the awareness of young adults, in the United Kingdom. A survey was sent to young adults in the United Kingdom - i.e., Dublin, Cambridge, Scotland. Sixteen young adults consented and completed the study. 6% were over the age of 22 years old, 6% were under the age of 18 years old, and the remaining 88% were split evenly across the two cohorts of "18-19 years old" and "20-22 years old". 63% were female, 44% knew of a family member

* Correspondence: Ronald Chow BMSc(C), Infinitas Research Group, London, Ontario, Canada. Email: rchow48@uwo.ca.

affected by ASD, and 38% knew of a friend affected by ASD. 38% were aware of ASD; 38% of the young adults surveyed had a friend affected by ASD, and 44% had a family member affected by ASD. The data suggests that future prevalence may be approximately equal to current awareness, as the statistics are rather similar. Future longitudinal studies should look into evaluating the future prevalence.

INTRODUCTION

The awareness of young adults with respect to autism spectrum disorder (ASD) has been studied, as it has been suggested that the awareness of parents affects the number of diagnosed cases - there is a positive correlation between awareness and prevalence of ASD (1-2). The original study by Chow et al. studied young adults in London, Canada, and found that 56% were aware of ASD, 26% had a family member with ASD and 44% had a friend with ASD (3). The future prevalence, as interpreted from data in this study, may potentially be greater than today.

Follow-up studies were conducted among young adults in other regions of North America - Toronto (4), California (5), Montreal (6) and Calgary (7). These studies found that the proportion of individuals aware of ASD is an intermediate value of the proportion of individuals knowing a family member with ASD, and the proportion of individuals who know a friend with ASD. All four studies suggested that future prevalence may actually be similar to the current prevalence.

There was tremendous variation between the studies, and no study has been performed yet to evaluate the awareness of young adults outside of North America. The aim of our study was to further look into the awareness of young adults, in the United Kingdom.

OUR STUDY

A three-page survey was sent to young adults in the United Kingdom - i.e., Dublin, Cambridge, Scotland. The first page had a consent form listing the benefits/costs, and required participants to consent in order to complete the questionnaire. The second page collected participant demographics, and the third page assessed the perceived knowledge of ASD and also contained eight assessment questions (8).

Descriptive statistics were used to convey participant demographics, and also the responses provided by participants. Fisher exact tests were run to investigate whether different subgroups provided different responses. Subgroup analyses were conducted by age group (under/over 20 years old), sex (males/females), whether they have a family member with ASD, and whether they have a friend with ASD. P-values less than 0.05 were considered statistically significant. All statistical procedures were conducted using the Statistical Analysis Software (SAS Version 9.4 for Windows) (8).

FINDINGS

Sixteen young adults consented and completed the study. 6% were over the age of 22 years old, 6% were under the age of 18 years old, and the remaining 88% were split evenly across the two cohorts of "18-19 years old" and "20-22 years old". 63% were female, 44% knew of a family member affected by ASD, and 38% knew of a friend affected by ASD (see Table 1).

38% perceived themselves as knowledgeable about ASD. All respondents correctly identified that ASD is a lifelong developmental condition, and that it is not caused by poor parenting. 69% noted that its prevalence has increased over the years, 81% indicated that it does not arise from vaccinations, 81% answered that individuals do not always prefer to be alone, 69% reported that not all people are eccentric geniuses, 63% remarked that individuals cannot grow out of it, and 44% said that patients do not require substantial medical assistance. Overall, 38% of respondents were knowledgeable about ASD (see Table 2).

When comparing respondents of different age cohorts, there was no difference in the perceived awareness - 25% of those under 20 years old and 50% of those over 20 years old believed they were knowledgeable about ASD ($p = 0.2821$). 100% and 100% of the two groups, respectively, answered that it is a lifelong developmental condition ($p = 0.9999$) and that it is not caused by poor parenting ($p = 0.9999$). 88% and 50% disagreed to the statement that "the prevalence of autism has increased over the years" ($p = 0.0769$), 100% and 63% to "autism can arise from vaccinations" ($p = 0.2000$), 100% and 63% to "individuals with autism always prefer to be alone" ($p = 0.2000$), 88% and 50% to "people with autism are eccentric geniuses" ($p = 0.2000$), 63% and 63% to "individuals with autism can grow out of it" ($p = 0.9999$) and 50% and 38% to "people with autism require substantial medical assistance" ($p = 0.6737$). Those under 20 years old were more knowledgeable ($p = 0.0070$) - 75% were knowledgeable, compared to 0% of individuals over 20 years old (see Table 3).

Table 1. Demographics

Demographic	**n = 16**
Age Group	
Under 18 years old	1 (6%)
18-19 years old	7 (44%)
20-22 years old	7 (44%)
Over 22 years old	1 (6%)
Sex	
Male	6 (38%)
Female	10 (63%)
Prefer not to say	0 (0%)
Family member affected by Autism	
Yes	7 (44%)
No	9 (56%)
Friend(s) affected by Autism	
Yes	6 (38%)
No	10 (63%)

Table 2. Perceived and actual knowledge

Question Item	n = 16
"I believe I am knowledgeable about Autism"	
Agree	6 (38%)
Disagree	3 (19%)
Neutral	7 (44%)
"Autism is a life-long developmental condition"	
True	16 (100%)
False	0 (0%)
Not Sure	0 (0%)
"Autism can be caused by poor parenting or parental behavior"	
True	0 (0%)
False	16 (100%)
Not Sure	0 (0%)
"The prevalence of Autism has increased over the years"	
True	11 (69%)
False	1 (6%)
Not Sure	4 (25%)
"Autism can arise from vaccinations"	
True	0 (0%)
False	13 (81%)
Not Sure	3 (19%)
"Individuals with Autism always prefer to be alone"	
True	2 (13%)
False	13 (81%)
Not Sure	1 (6%)
"People with Autism are eccentric geniuses"	
True	3 (19%)
False	11 (69%)
Not Sure	2 (13%)
"Individuals with Autism can grow out of it"	
True	2 (13%)
False	10 (63%)
Not Sure	4 (25%)
"People with Autism require substantial medical assistance"	
True	4 (25%)
False	7 (44%)
Not Sure	5 (31%)
Knowledge Score	
Not Knowledgeable (0-4)	1 (6%)
Satisfactory (5-6)	9 (56%)
Knowledgeable (7-8)	6 (38%)

There was no difference in perceived (p = 0.9999) and actual awareness (p = 0.9999) between males and females. There also existed no difference in perceived awareness between those with and without family members affected by ASD (p = 0.2321), and actual awareness (p = 0.6145). When comparing those with and without friends affected by ASD, there was no difference in perceived (p = 0.9999) and actual (p = 0.5542) awareness (see Table 3).

Table 3. Perceived and actual knowledge - by subgroups

Question Item	**Under 20 n = 8**	**Over 20 n = 8**	**p-value**
"I believe I am knowledgeable about Autism"			0.2821
Agree	2 (25%)	4 (50%)	
Disagree	3 (38%)	0 (0%)	
Neutral	3 (38%)	4 (50%)	
"Autism is a life-long developmental condition"			0.9999
True	8 (100%)	8 (100%)	
False	0 (0%)	0 (0%)	
Not Sure	0 (0%)	0 (0%)	
"Autism can be caused by poor parenting or parental behavior"			0.9999
True	0 (0%)	0 (0%)	
False	8 (100%)	8 (100%)	
Not Sure	0 (0%)	0 (0%)	
"The prevalence of Autism has increased over the years"			0.0769
True	7 (88%)	4 (50%)	
False	1 (13%)	0 (0%)	
Not Sure	0 (0%)	4 (50%)	
"Autism can arise from vaccinations"			0.2000
True	0 (0%)	0 (0%)	
False	8 (100%)	5 (63%)	
Not Sure	0 (0%)	3 (38%)	
"Individuals with Autism always prefer to be alone"			0.2000
True	0 (0%)	2 (25%)	
False	8 (100%)	5 (63%)	
Not Sure	0 (0%)	1 (13%)	
"People with Autism are eccentric geniuses"			0.2000
True	0 (0%)	3 (38%)	
False	7 (88%)	4 (50%)	
Not Sure	1 (13%)	1 (13%)	

Question Item	Under 20 n = 8	Over 20 n = 8	p-value
"Individuals with Autism can grow out of it"			0.9999
True	1 (13%)	1 (13%)	
False	5 (63%)	5 (63%)	
Not Sure	2 (25%)	2 (25%)	
"People with Autism require substantial medical assistance"			0.6737
True	1 (13%)	3 (38%)	
False	4 (50%)	3 (38%)	
Not Sure	3 (38%)	2 (25%)	
Knowledge Score			0.0070
Not Knowledgeable (0-4)	0 (0%)	1 (13%)	
Satisfactory (5-6)	2 (25%)	7 (88%)	
Knowledgeable (7-8)	6 (75%)	0 (0%)	
Question Item	**Males n = 6**	**Females n = 10**	
"I believe I am knowledgeable about Autism"			0.9999
Agree	2 (33%)	4 (40%)	
Disagree	1 (17%)	2 (20%)	
Neutral	3 (50%)	4 (40%)	
"Autism is a life-long developmental condition"			0.9999
True	6 (100%)	10 (100%)	
False	0 (0%)	0 (0%)	
Not Sure	0 (0%)	0 (0%)	
"Autism can be caused by poor parenting or parental behavior"			0.9999
True	0 (0%)	0 (0%)	
False	6 (100%)	10 (100%)	
Not Sure	0 (0%)	0 (0%)	
"The prevalence of Autism has increased over the years"			0.9999
True	4 (67%)	7 (70%)	
False	0 (0%)	1 (10%)	
Not Sure	2 (33%)	2 (20%)	
"Autism can arise from vaccinations"			0.2500
True	0 (0%)	0 (0%)	
False	6 (100%)	7 (70%)	
Not Sure	0 (0%)	3 (30%)	
"Individuals with Autism always prefer to be alone"			0.9999
True	1 (17%)	1 (10%)	
False	5 (83%)	8 (80%)	
Not Sure	0 (0%)	1 (10%)	
"People with Autism are eccentric geniuses"			0.2170
True	1 (17%)	2 (20%)	
False	3 (50%)	8 (80%)	
Not Sure	2 (33%)	0 (0%)	

Table 3. (Continued)

Question Item	**Males n = 6**	**Females n = 10**	
"Individuals with Autism can grow out of it"			0.6104
True	0 (0%)	2 (20%)	
False	4 (67%)	6 (60%)	
Not Sure	2 (33%)	2 (20%)	
"People with Autism require substantial medical assistance"			0.5367
True	1 (17%)	3 (30%)	
False	2 (33%)	5 (50%)	
Not Sure	3 (50%)	2 (20%)	
Knowledge Score			0.9999
Not Knowledgeable (0-4)	0 (0%)	1 (10%)	
Satisfactory (5-6)	4 (67%)	5 (50%)	
Knowledgeable (7-8)	2 (33%)	4 (40%)	
Question Item	**Family affected n = 7**	**Family unaffected n = 9**	
"I believe I am knowledgeable about Autism"			0.2321
Agree	4 (57%)	2 (22%)	
Disagree	0 (0%)	3 (33%)	
Neutral	3 (43%)	4 (44%)	
"Autism is a life-long developmental condition"			0.9999
True	7 (100%)	9 (100%)	
False	0 (0%)	0 (0%)	
Not Sure	0 (0%)	0 (0%)	
"Autism can be caused by poor parenting or parental behavior"			0.9999
True	0 (0%)	0 (0%)	
False	7 (100%)	9 (100%)	
Not Sure	0 (0%)	0 (0%)	
"The prevalence of Autism has increased over the years"			0.9999
True	5 (71%)	6 (67%)	
False	0 (0%)	1 (11%)	
Not Sure	2 (29%)	2 (22%)	
"Autism can arise from vaccinations"			0.0625
True	0 (0%)	0 (0%)	
False	4 (57%)	9 (100%)	
Not Sure	3 (43%)	0 (0%)	
"Individuals with Autism always prefer to be alone"			0.9999
True	1 (14%)	1 (11%)	
False	6 (86%)	7 (78%)	
Not Sure	0 (0%)	1 (11%)	

Question Item	Family affected n = 7	Family unaffected n = 9	
"People with Autism are eccentric geniuses"			0.9999
True	1 (14%)	2 (22%)	
False	5 (71%)	6 (67%)	
Not Sure	1 (14%)	1 (11%)	
"Individuals with Autism can grow out of it"			0.7797
True	1 (14%)	1 (11%)	
False	5 (71%)	5 (56%)	
Not Sure	1 (14%)	3 (33%)	
"People with Autism require substantial medical assistance"			0.9999
True	2 (29%)	2 (22%)	
False	3 (43%)	4 (44%)	
Not Sure	2 (29%)	3 (33%)	
Knowledge Score			0.6145
Not Knowledgeable (0-4)	0 (0%)	1 (11%)	
Satisfactory (5-6)	5 (71%)	4 (44%)	
Knowledgeable (7-8)	2 (29%)	4 (44%)	
Question Item	**Friend affected n = 6**	**Friend unaffected n = 10**	
"I believe I am knowledgeable about Autism"			0.9999
Agree	2 (33%)	4 (40%)	
Disagree	1 (17%)	2 (20%)	
Neutral	3 (50%)	4 (40%)	
"Autism is a life-long developmental condition"			0.9999
True	6 (100%)	10 (100%)	
False	0 (0%)	0 (0%)	
Not Sure	0 (0%)	0 (0%)	
"Autism can be caused by poor parenting or parental behavior"			0.9999
True	0 (0%)	0 (0%)	
False	6 (100%)	10 (100%)	
Not Sure	0 (0%)	0 (0%)	
"The prevalence of Autism has increased over the years"			0.9999
True	4 (67%)	7 (70%)	
False	0 (0%)	1 (10%)	
Not Sure	2 (33%)	2 (20%)	
"Autism can arise from vaccinations"			0.5179
True	0 (0%)	0 (0%)	
False	4 (67%)	9 (90%)	
Not Sure	2 (33%)	1 (10%)	

Table 3. (Continued)

Question Item	**Friend affected n = 6**	**Friend unaffected n = 10**	
"Individuals with Autism always prefer to be alone"			0.2857
True	0 (0%)	2 (20%)	
False	5 (83%)	8 (80%)	
Not Sure	1 (17%)	0 (0%)	
"People with Autism are eccentric geniuses"			0.9999
True	1 (17%)	2 (20%)	
False	4 (67%)	7 (70%)	
Not Sure	1 (17%)	1 (10%)	
"Individuals with Autism can grow out of it"			0.3272
True	1 (17%)	1 (10%)	
False	5 (83%)	5 (50%)	
Not Sure	0 (0%)	4 (40%)	
"People with Autism require substantial medical assistance"			0.3444
True	3 (50%)	1 (10%)	
False	2 (33%)	5 (50%)	
Not Sure	1 (17%)	4 (40%)	
Knowledge Score			0.5542
Not Knowledgeable (0-4)	1 (17%)	0 (0%)	
Satisfactory (5-6)	3 (50%)	6 (60%)	
Knowledgeable (7-8)	2 (33%)	4 (40%)	

DISCUSSION

38% of young adults were knowledgeable about ASD. 44% had a family member affected, and 38% had a friend affected. The data suggests that future prevalence may be approximately equal to current awareness, as the statistics are rather similar. Future longitudinal studies should look into evaluating the future prevalence.

Those under 20 years old seemed to be more knowledgeable than those over 20 years old. This could be a result of the greater prevalence during the upbringing of the younger individuals, and consequently a higher exposure to ASD individuals. However, there was a lack of difference in knowledge between those with and without affected friends/family members, which may seem to suggest that exposure may not be indicative of actual awareness.

This study was not without limitations, especially due to the low number of respondents. As it is a survey study, there exists the possibility of a response and sampling bias. Data was reviewed to identify any anomalies, and none were found, hopefully reducing the possibility of a response bias.

In conclusion, 38% were aware of ASD. 38% of the young adults surveyed had a friend affected by ASD, and 44% had a family member affected by ASD. The data suggests that future prevalence may be approximately equal to current awareness, as the statistics are rather similar. Future longitudinal studies should look into evaluating the future prevalence.

Acknowledgment

We would like to thank Drew Hollenberg for the support.

References

[1] Fombonne E, Zakarian R, Bennett A, Meng L, McLean-Heywood D. Pervasive developmental disorders in Montreal, Quebec, Canada: Prevalence and links with immunization. Pediatrics 2006;118:e139-50.

[2] Shattuck PT. The combination of diagnostic substitution to the growing administrative prevalence of autism in US special education data. Pediatrics 2006;117:1028-37.

[3] Chow R, Viehweger J, Anpalagan T, Yang H, Banerjee R. Awareness of autism spectrum disorder among young adults in London, Canada. Int Public Health J 2019;11(1), in press.

[4] Chow R, Viehweger J, Hollenberg D, Ho C, Ng W, Wong M. Awareness of autism spectrum disorder among young adults in Toronto, Canada. Int Public Health J 2019;11(1), in press.

[5] Chow R, Viehweger J, Murai A. Awareness of autism spectrum disorder among young adults in California, USA. Int Public Health J 2019;11(1), in press.

[6] Viehweger J, Chow R, Borean M. Awareness of autism spectrum disorder among young adults in Montreal, Canada. Int Public Health J 2019;11(1), in press.

[7] Chow R, Viehweger J. Awareness of autism spectrum disorder among young adults in Calgary, Canada. Int Public Health J 2019;11(1), in press.

[8] Chow R, Viehweger J. Assessing awareness of autism spectrum disorder: about the survey instrument. Int Public Health J 2019;11(1), in press.

In: Autism Spectrum Disorder ISBN: 978-1-53612-730-0
Editors: R. Chow, J. Viehweger et al. ©2017 Nova Science Publishers, Inc.

Chapter 12

AWARENESS OF AUTISM SPECTRUM DISORDER AMONG YOUNG ADULTS IN ASIA

Jaclyn Viehweger, BMSc(C)
and Ronald Chow*, BMSc(C)
Infinitas Research Group, London, Ontario, Canada

In this chapter our aim was to assess the awareness of young adults in Asia. A questionnaire was sent to young adults in Asia (i.e., Taiwan, Hong Kong, Singapore). The first page of three pages had a consent form listing the benefits/costs, and required participants to consent in order to complete the questionnaire. The second page collected participant demographics, and the third page assessed the perceived knowledge of ASD and also contained eight assessment questions. Descriptive statistics were used to convey participant demographics, and also the responses provided by participants. Fisher exact tests were run to investigate whether different subgroups provided different responses. Subgroup analyses were conducted by age group (under/over 20 years old), sex (males/females), whether they have a family member with ASD, and whether they have a friend with ASD. P-values less than 0.05 were considered statistically significant. All statistical procedures were conducted using the Statistical Analysis Software (SAS Version 9.4 for

* Correspondence: Ronald Chow BMSc(C), Infinitas Research Group, London, Ontario, Canada. Email: rchow48@uwo.ca.

Windows). 67% were knowledgeable about ASD, which is well in excess of the 38% of those who had a family member affected and 48% that had a friend affected. As this study has a smaller sample size than previously published literature, this finding may simply be an anomaly of the smaller sample size. Of the subgroup analyses, there was only a difference in knowledge between males and females. This may be a result of the different culture in Asia, which places a greater emphasis on males to be knowledgeable and care for diseases and disorders in the community.

INTRODUCTION

The number of diagnosed cases of ASD has been reported to be related with the awareness of ASD among parents - the greater the awareness, the greater the number of diagnosed cases (1, 2).

Survey studies have been conducted to investigate into the awareness of young adults with respect to ASD. By investigating young adults (the parents of the near-future), hopefully one could gain insight into the future number of diagnosed ASD cases. Studies in London (Canada) (3), Toronto (4), CAlifornia (5), Montreal (6), Calgary (7), the United Kingdom (8) and New York State (9) have reported that future prevalence may be similar to current prevalence - however, more rigorous longitudinal studies should be conducted. Nevertheless, the published literature has also revealed that there is significant deviance amongst the data by geographic region. Our aim was to assess the awareness of young adults in Asia.

THE STUDY

A questionnaire was sent to young adults in Asia (i.e., Taiwan, Hong Kong, Singapore). The first page of three pages had a consent form listing the benefits/costs, and required participants to consent in order to complete the questionnaire. The second page collected participant demographics, and the third page assessed the perceived knowledge of ASD and also contained eight assessment questions (10).

Descriptive statistics were used to convey participant demographics, and also the responses provided by participants. Fisher exact tests were run to investigate whether different subgroups provided different responses. Subgroup analyses were conducted by age group (under/over 20 years old), sex (males/females), whether they have a family member with ASD, and whether they have a friend with ASD. P-values less than 0.05 were considered statistically significant. All statistical procedures were conducted using the Statistical Analysis Software (SAS Version 9.4 for Windows) (10).

The findings

Of the 21 respondents, 3 (14%) were under the age of 18 years old, and the remaining 18 were evenly distributed between the age groups of 18-19 years old, 20-22 years old and over 22 years old (29% per each group). 10% did not identify their sex - 62% were female and 29% were male. 38% had a family member affected by ASD, and 48% knew of a friend affected by ASD (see Table 1).

57% of young adults believed they were knowledgeable about ASD. 86% and 81% remarked affirmative to the following two statements: "Autism is a life-long developmental condition" and "the prevalence of Autism has increased over the years." 95% noted that it cannot be caused by poor parenting, 90% remarked that it cannot arise from vaccinations, 90% indicated that individuals do not always prefer to be alone, 86% answered that people are not eccentric geniuses, 76% concluded that they cannot grow out of it, and 57% answered that patients do not require substantial medical assistance. Overall, 67% of young adults were knowledgeable (see Table 2).

Table 1. Demographics

Demographic	n = 21
Age Group	
Under 18 years old	3 (14%)
18-19 years old	6 (29%)
20-22 years old	6 (29%)
Over 22 years old	6 (29%)
Sex	
Male	6 (29%)
Female	13 (62%)
Prefer not to say	2 (10%)
Family member affected by Autism	
Yes	8 (38%)
No	13 (62%)
Friend(s) affected by Autism	
Yes	10 (48%)
No	11 (52%)

Table 2. Perceived and actual knowledge

Question Item	n = 21
"I believe I am knowledgeable about Autism"	
Agree	12 (57%)
Disagree	2 (10%)
Neutral	7 (33%)
"Autism is a life-long developmental condition"	
True	18 (86%)
False	2 (10%)
Not Sure	1 (5%)
"Autism can be caused by poor parenting or parental behavior"	
True	0 (0%)
False	20 (95%)
Not Sure	1 (5%)
"The prevalence of Autism has increased over the years"	
True	17 (81%)
False	0 (0%)
Not Sure	4 (19%)

Question Item	**n = 21**
"Autism can arise from vaccinations"	
True	0 (0%)
False	19 (90%)
Not Sure	2 (10%)
"Individuals with Autism always prefer to be alone"	
True	1 (5%)
False	19 (90%)
Not Sure	1 (5%)
"People with Autism are eccentric geniuses"	
True	1 (5%)
False	18 (86%)
Not Sure	2 (10%)
"Individuals with Autism can grow out of it"	
True	3 (14%)
False	16 (76%)
Not Sure	2 (10%)
"People with Autism require substantial medical assistance"	
True	4 (19%)
False	12 (57%)
Not Sure	5 (24%)
Knowledge Score	
Not Knowledgeable (0-4)	1 (5%)
Satisfactory (5-6)	6 (29%)
Knowledgeable (7-8)	14 (67%)

There was no difference in perceived (p=0.2982) and actual (p=0.9999) awareness between those under and over 20 years old. 89% and 83% noted that it is a life-long developmental condition (p=0.3203) and 100% and 92% that it is not caused by poor parenting (p=0.9999). 67% and 92% answered that its prevalence has increased over the years (p=0.2722), 100% and 83% that it cannot arise from vaccinations (p=0.4857), 100% and 83% that individuals do not always prefer to be alone (p=0.9999), and 78% and 92% that not all individuals are eccentric geniuses (p=0.7023). 67% and 83% noted that individuals cannot grow out of it (p=0.7665), and 78% and 42% indicated that patients do not require substantial medical assistance (p=0.3421) (see Table 3).

Table 3. Perceived and actual knowledge - by subgroups

Question Item	Under 20 n = 9	Over 20 n = 12	p-value
"I believe I am knowledgeable about Autism"			0.2982
Agree	5 (56%)	7 (58%)	
Disagree	2 (22%)	0 (0%)	
Neutral	2 (22%)	5 (42%)	
"Autism is a life-long developmental condition"			0.3203
True	8 (89%)	10 (83%)	
False	0 (0%)	2 (17%)	
Not Sure	1 (11%)	0 (0%)	
"Autism can be caused by poor parenting or parental behavior"			0.9999
True	0 (0%)	0 (0%)	
False	9 (100%)	11 (92%)	
Not Sure	0 (0%)	1 (8%)	
"The prevalence of Autism has increased over the years"			0.2722
True	6 (67%)	11 (92%)	
False	0 (0%)	0 (0%)	
Not Sure	3 (33%)	1 (8%)	
"Autism can arise from vaccinations"			0.4857
True	0 (0%)	0 (0%)	
False	9 (100%)	10 (83%)	
Not Sure	0 (0%)	2 (17%)	
"Individuals with Autism always prefer to be alone"			0.9999
True	0 (0%)	1 (8%)	
False	9 (100%)	10 (83%)	
Not Sure	0 (0%)	1 (8%)	
"People with Autism are eccentric geniuses"			0.7023
True	1 (11%)	0 (0%)	
False	7 (78%)	11 (92%)	
Not Sure	1 (11%)	1 (8%)	

Question Item	Under 20 n = 9	Over 20 n = 12	p-value
"Individuals with Autism can grow out of it"			0.7665
True	2 (22%)	1 (8%)	
False	6 (67%)	10 (83%)	
Not Sure	1 (11%)	1 (8%)	
"People with Autism require substantial medical assistance"			0.3421
True	1 (11%)	3 (25%)	
False	7 (78%)	5 (42%)	
Not Sure	1 (11%)	4 (33%)	
Knowledge Score			0.9999
Not Knowledgeable (0-4)	0 (0%)	1 (8%)	
Satisfactory (5-6)	3 (33%)	3 (25%)	
Knowledgeable (7-8)	6 (67%)	8 (67%)	
Question Item	**Males n = 6**	**Females n = 13**	
"I believe I am knowledgeable about Autism"			0.8143
Agree	4 (67%)	6 (46%)	
Disagree	0 (0%)	2 (15%)	
Neutral	2 (33%)	5 (38%)	
"Autism is a life-long developmental condition"			0.6780
True	6 (100%)	10 (77%)	
False	0 (0%)	2 (15%)	
Not Sure	0 (0%)	1 (8%)	
"Autism can be caused by poor parenting or parental behavior"			0.9999
True	0 (0%)	0 (0%)	
False	5 (83%)	12 (92%)	
Not Sure	1 (17%)	1 (8%)	
"The prevalence of Autism has increased over the years"			0.9999
True	5 (83%)	10 (77%)	
False	0 (0%)	0 (0%)	
Not Sure	1 (17%)	3 (23%)	
"Autism can arise from vaccinations"			0.9999
True	0 (0%)	0 (0%)	
False	6 (100%)	11 (85%)	
Not Sure	0 (0%)	2 (15%)	

Table 3. (Continued)

Question Item	**Males n = 6**	**Females n = 13**	
"Individuals with Autism always prefer to be alone"			0.5439
True	1 (17%)	0 (0%)	
False	5 (83%)	12 (92%)	
Not Sure	0 (0%)	1 (8%)	
"People with Autism are eccentric geniuses"			0.9999
True	0 (0%)	1 (8%)	
False	5 (83%)	11 (85%)	
Not Sure	1 (17%)	1 (8%)	
"Individuals with Autism can grow out of it"			0.9999
True	1 (17%)	2 (15%)	
False	4 (67%)	10 (77%)	
Not Sure	1 (17%)	1 (8%)	
"People with Autism require substantial medical assistance"			0.8054
True	2 (33%)	2 (15%)	
False	3 (50%)	8 (62%)	
Not Sure	1 (17%)	3 (23%)	
Knowledge Score			0.0387
Not Knowledgeable (0-4)	1 (17%)	0 (0%)	
Satisfactory (5-6)	0 (0%)	6 (46%)	
Knowledgeable (7-8)	5 (83%)	7 (54%)	
Question Item	**Family affected n = 8**	**Family unaffected n = 13**	
"I believe I am knowledgeable about Autism"			0.5300
Agree	6 (75%)	6 (46%)	
Disagree	0 (0%)	2 (15%)	
Neutral	2 (25%)	5 (38%)	
"Autism is a life-long developmental condition"			0.6872
True	8 (100%)	10 (77%)	
False	0 (0%)	2 (15%)	
Not Sure	0 (0%)	1 (8%)	

Question Item	**Family affected n = 8**	**Family unaffected n = 13**	
"Autism can be caused by poor parenting or parental behavior"			0.3810
True	0 (0%)	0 (0%)	
False	7 (88%)	13 (100%)	
Not Sure	1 (13%)	0 (0%)	
"The prevalence of Autism has increased over the years"			0.9999
True	7 (88%)	10 (77%)	
False	0 (0%)	0 (0%)	
Not Sure	1 (13%)	3 (23%)	
"Autism can arise from vaccinations"			0.9999
True	0 (0%)	0 (0%)	
False	7 (88%)	12 (92%)	
Not Sure	1 (13%)	1 (8%)	
"Individuals with Autism always prefer to be alone"			0.1333
True	1 (13%)	0 (0%)	
False	6 (25%)	13 (100%)	
Not Sure	1 (13%)	0 (0%)	
"People with Autism are eccentric geniuses"			0.9999
True	0 (0%)	1 (8%)	
False	7 (88%)	11 (85%)	
Not Sure	1 (13%)	1 (8%)	
"Individuals with Autism can grow out of it"			0.9999
True	1 (13%)	2 (15%)	
False	6 (75%)	10 (77%)	
Not Sure	1 (13%)	1 (8%)	
"People with Autism require substantial medical assistance"			0.2346
True	3 (38%)	1 (8%)	
False	3 (38%)	9 (69%)	
Not Sure	2 (25%)	3 (23%)	
Knowledge Score			0.5819
Not Knowledgeable (0-4)	1 (13%)	0 (0%)	
Satisfactory (5-6)	2 (25%)	4 (31%)	
Knowledgeable (7-8)	5 (63%)	9 (69%)	

Table 3. (Continued)

Question Item	**Friend affected n = 10**	**Friend unaffected n = 11**	
"I believe I am knowledgeable about Autism"			0.4734
Agree	7 (70%)	5 (45%)	
Disagree	0 (0%)	2 (18%)	
Neutral	3 (30%)	4 (36%)	
"Autism is a life-long developmental condition"			0.9999
True	9 (90%)	9 (82%)	
False	1 (10%)	1 (9%)	
Not Sure	0 (0%)	1 (9%)	
"Autism can be caused by poor parenting or parental behavior"			0.4762
True	0 (0%)	0 (0%)	
False	9 (90%)	11 (100%)	
Not Sure	1 (10%)	0 (0%)	
"The prevalence of Autism has increased over the years"			0.9999
True	8 (80%)	9 (82%)	
False	0 (0%)	0 (0%)	
Not Sure	2 (20%)	2 (18%)	
"Autism can arise from vaccinations"			0.4762
True	0 (0%)	0 (0%)	
False	10 (100%)	9 (82%)	
Not Sure	0 (0%)	2 (18%)	
"Individuals with Autism always prefer to be alone"			0.2143
True	1 (10%)	0 (0%)	
False	8 (80%)	11 (100%)	
Not Sure	1 (10%)	0 (0%)	
"People with Autism are eccentric geniuses"			0.3383
True	0 (0%)	1 (9%)	
False	8 (80%)	10 (91%)	
Not Sure	2 (20%)	0 (0%)	

Question Item	**Friend affected n = 10**	**Friend unaffected n = 11**	
"Individuals with Autism can grow out of it"			0.4770
True	1 (10%)	2 (18%)	
False	9 (90%)	7 (64%)	
Not Sure	0 (0%)	2 (18%)	
"People with Autism require substantial medical assistance"			0.9999
True	2 (20%)	2 (18%)	
False	6 (60%)	6 (55%)	
Not Sure	2 (20%)	3 (27%)	
Knowledge Score			0.1486
Not Knowledgeable (0-4)	1 (10%)	0 (0%)	
Satisfactory (5-6)	1 (10%)	5 (45%)	
Knowledgeable (7-8)	8 (80%)	6 (55%)	

Perceived awareness did not differ between the males and females (p=0.8143) - 67% and 46%, respectively, believed they were knowledgeable about ASD. 100% and 77% (p=0.6780), and 83% and 77% (p=0.9999), answered "True" to the statements "Autism is a life-long developmental condition" and "the prevalence of Autism has increased over the years," respectively. 83% and 92% remarked that it cannot be caused by poor parenting (p=0.9999), 100% and 85% that it cannot arise from vaccinations (p=0.9999), 83% and 92% that individuals do not always prefer to be alone (p=0.5439), 83% and 85% that not all individuals are eccentric geniuses (p=0.9999), 67% and 77% that they cannot grow out of it (p=0.9999), and 50% and 62% that they do not require substantial medical assistance (p=0.8054). Overall, males were more knowledgeable about ASD than females (83% sv 54%; p=0.0387) (see Table 3).

Studying perceived awareness between those with and without a family member affected by ASD, there was no difference (p=0.5300). There was also no difference in perceived awareness between participants with and without affected friends (p=0.4734). The actual awareness of the two subgroup analyses also found no difference between the groups (p=0.5819, and p=0.1486, respectively) (see Table 3).

Discussion

This study has a smaller sample size than previously published literature (3-9). 67% were knowledgeable, which is well in excess of the 38% who had a family member affected and 48% who had a friend affected - this finding may simply be an anomaly of the smaller sample size.

The subgroup analyses indicated that males were more knowledgeable than females, which was not previously reported. This may be a result of the different culture in Asia, which places a greater emphasis on males to be knowledgeable and care for diseases and disorders in the community. There were no other differences between the subgroups, which confirms prior studies (3-9).

This study was not without limitations. As it is a survey, sampling and response biases can occur and especially with the low number of respondents. To mitigate this, we looked at individual responses to assess whether there were any abnormal responses (i.e., 8 responses that seemed to be purposely wrong).

In conclusion, 67% were knowledgeable about ASD, which is well in excess of the 38% of those who had a family member affected and 48% that had a friend affected. As this study has a smaller sample size than previously published literature, this finding may simply be an anomaly of the smaller sample size. Of the subgroup analyses, there was only a difference in knowledge between males and females. This may be a result of the different culture in Asia, which places a greater emphasis on males to be knowledgeable and care for diseases and disorders in the community.

References

[1] Fombonne E, Zakarian R, Bennett A, Meng L, McLean-Heywood D. Pervasive developmental disorders in Montreal, Quebec, Canada: Prevalence and links with immunization. Pediatrics 2006;118:e139-50.

[2] Shattuck PT. The combination of diagnostic substitution to the growing administrative prevalence of autism in US special education data. Pediatrics 2006;117:1028-37.

[3] Chow R, Viehweger J, Anpalagan T, Yang H, Banerjee R. Awareness of autism spectrum disorder among young adults in London, Canada. Int Public Health J 2019;11(1), in press.
[4] Chow R, Viehweger J, Hollenberg D, Ho C, Ng W, Wong M. Awareness of autism spectrum disorder among young adults in Toronto, Canada. Int Public Health J 2019;11(1), in press.
[5] Chow R, Viehweger J, Murai A. Awareness of autism spectrum disorder among young adults in California, USA. Int Public Health J 2019;11(1), in press.
[6] Viehweger J, Chow R, Borean M. Awareness of autism spectrum disorder among young adults in Montreal, Canada. Int Public Health J 2019;11(1), in press.
[7] Chow R, Viehweger J. Awareness of autism spectrum disorder among young adults in Calgary, Canada. Int Public Health J 2019;11(1), in press.
[8] Viehweger J, Chow R, Goh S. Awareness of autism spectrum disorder among young adults in United Kingdom. Int Public Health J 2019;11(1), in press.
[9] Viehweger J, Chow R, Ganguli N. Awareness of autism spectrum disorder among young adults in New York State, USA. Int Public Health J 2019;11(1), in press.
[10] Chow R, Viehweger J. Assessing awareness of autism spectrum disorder: About the survey instrument. Int Public Health J 2019;11(1), in press.

SECTION THREE: OVERALL AWARENESS

In: Autism Spectrum Disorder ISBN: 978-1-53612-730-0
Editors: R. Chow, J. Viehweger et al. ©2017 Nova Science Publishers, Inc.

Chapter 13

HOW AWARE ARE YOUNG ADULTS OF AUTISM SPECTRUM DISORDER? A META-ANALYSIS

Ronald Chow**, BMSc(C)
and Jaclyn Viehweger, BMSc(C)
Infinitas Research Group, London, Ontario, Canada

Numerous studies have surveyed young adults across the globe to assess the awareness of autism spectrum disorder (ASD), however, there yet exists a study pooling together all of the data. The aim of this meta-analysis was to synthesize conclusions from amalgamated data. The same endpoints as reported in the studies were extracted from each study, and summed together. Descriptive statistics were used to report the characteristics of included studies, the demographics of all respondents, and also the responses to survey questions to assess perceived and actual awareness. Subgroup analyses were conducted to examine whether knowledge differs by age (under 20 years old vs over 20 years old), sex (males vs females), familial ties (knowing of a family member with ASD vs not knowing of a family member with ASD) and exposure to friends (knowing of a friend with ASD vs not knowing of a friend with ASD). Chi-square tests were used to statistically determine whether there existed a difference. 48% believed they were knowledgeable about ASD. A

* Correspondence: Ronald Chow BMSc(C), Infinitas Research Group, London, Ontario, Canada. Email: rchow48@uwo.ca.

greater proportion had a friend who knew of a friend affected by ASD (52%) and a smaller proportion knew of a family member affected by ASD (34%). The subgroup analyses indicates that exposure to a friend may be related to greater awareness, revealing that knowing of an individual afflicted by ASD may increase awareness. Future studies should follow young adults to chart whether the future prevalence remains the same, as suggested by our results.

INTRODUCTION

Autism spectrum disorder (ASM) is an umbrella term for a range of neurological disorders that presents with two types of symptoms: deficits in social communication and social interaction, and restricted, repetitive patterns of behaviours, interests or activities (1). ASD, as specified in DSM-5, encompasses all diagnoses of autism, Asperger syndrome, pervasive developmental disorder not otherwise specified (PDD-NOS) and childhood disintegrative disorder (2).

The cause of ASD is unknown, with some suggesting it is a result of genetic composition and others noting that it could be caused by comorbidities such as tuberous sclerosis, fragile X syndrome, phenylketonuria and rubella (2-7). What is known is that the prevalence and number of diagnosed cases has increased over the past several decades, and this has been attributed to increase awareness of ASD among the public and parents (8-13).

Studying the awareness of ASD among today's young adults (tomorrow's parents) may allow for extrapolation of the future prevalence of ASD (14). Numerous studies (15-24) have surveyed young adults across the globe to assess the awareness, however, there yet exists a study pooling together all of the data. The aim of this meta-analysis was to synthesize conclusions from amalgamated data.

Our study

The same endpoints as reported in the studies (15-24) were extracted from each study, and summed together. Descriptive statistics were used to report the characteristics of included studies, the demographics of all respondents, and also the responses to survey questions to assess perceived and actual awareness. Subgroup analyses were conducted to examine whether knowledge differs by age (under 20 years old vs over 20 years old), sex (males vs females), familial ties (knowing of a family member with ASD vs not knowing of a family member with ASD) and exposure to friends (knowing of a friend with ASD vs not knowing of a friend with ASD). Chi-square tests were used to statistically determine whether there existed a difference. A p-value less than 0.05 was considered statistically significant. All analyses were conducted the Statistical Analysis Software (SAS Version 9.4).

What we found

A total of 10 studies were included in this meta-analysis (15-24). Six of the studies were conducted in Canada, two in the United States, one in the United Kingdom, and one in Asia. Study population ranged from 16 participants to 85, and the total population size for this meta-analysis was 332 (see Table 1).

The largest proportion of participants identified they were 18-19 years old (43%), while 31% were 20-22 years old, 15% were over 22 years old, and 11% were under 18 years old. Three-quarters of participants were female, 22% were male, and 4% did not identify their sex. 34% knew of a family member affected by ASD, and 52% knew of a friend affected by ASD (see Table 2).

Table 1. Characteristics of included studies

Study	Location	Study Population
Chow et al. (15)	London, Canada	50
Chow et al. (16)	Toronto, Canada	85
Chow et al. (17)	California, United States of America	28
Viehweger et al. (18)	Montreal, Canada	31
Chow et al. (19)	Calgary, Canada	30
Viehweger et al. (20)	United Kingdom	16
Viehweger et al. (21)	New York State, United States of America	24
Viehweger et al. (22)	Asia	21
Viehweger et al. (23)	Waterloo, Canada	25
Hollenberg et al. (24)	Hamilton, Canada	22
TOTAL		332

Table 2. Participant demographics

Demographic	n = 332
Age Group	
Under 18 years old	35 (11%)
18-19 years old	142 (43%)
20-22 years old	104 (31%)
Over 22 years old	51 (15%)
Sex	
Male	72 (22%)
Female	248 (75%)
Prefer not to say	12 (4%)
Family member affected by Autism	
Yes	112 (34%)
No	220 (66%)
Friend(s) affected by Autism	
Yes	173 (52%)
No	159 (48%)

The proportion who perceived themselves knowledgeable (49%) and who were actually knowledgeable (48%) were approximately similar. 87% remarked that it is a lifelong developmental condition, and 91% noted that it cannot be caused by poor parenting. 63% and 86% answered that the prevalence has increased over the year and that it cannot arise from vaccinations. 86% indicated that individuals do not always prefer to be alone, and 73% responded that not all ASD people are eccentric geniuses. 70% concluded that individuals cannot grow out of it, and 52% noted that people do not require substantial medical assistance (see Table 3).

Those over 20 years old perceived themselves to be more aware than those under 20 years old ($p = 0.0002$). Overall knowledge, however, did not differ between the groups ($p = 0.1529$). The older group were more likely to correctly answer that ASD cannot arise from vaccinations ($p = 0.0012$) and that not all individuals are eccentric geniuses ($p = 0.0015$) (see Table 4).

There was no difference in perceived awareness between males and females ($p = 0.2506$). Males and females did not answer assessment questions differently, and overall knowledge between the two groups were approximately similar ($p = 0.9155$) (see Table 4).

Those who knew of a family member affected by ASD were more likely to perceive themselves as knowledgeable ($p < 0.0001$). They were only more knowledgeable in one question ($p = 0.0121$) and actually were less knowledgeable about another question ($p = 0.0394$). Actual awareness did not differ between the two groups ($p = 0.0949$) (see Table 4).

Those who knew of a friend with ASD both perceived themselves as more knowledgeable ($p = 0.0028$) and were more knowledgeable ($p = 0.0118$). This group was more likely to correctly answer that it does not arise from vaccinations ($p = 0.0482$) and that individuals cannot grow out of it ($p = 0.0385$) (see Table 4).

DISCUSSION

This meta-analysis is the first to amalgamate all of the published data looking into the awareness of ASD. The results reveal that the self-assessment of awareness is relatively accurate in this setting - the percentage of people who believe they are aware and the percentage of people who are actually aware are similar.

Table 3. Perceived and actual knowledge

Question Item	n = 332
"I believe I am knowledgeable about Autism"	
Agree	163 (49%)
Disagree	33 (10%)
Neutral	136 (41%)
"Autism is a life-long developmental condition"	
True	290 (87%)
False	10 (3%)
Not Sure	32 (10%)
"Autism can be caused by poor parenting or parental behavior"	
True	4 (1%)
False	301 (91%)
Not Sure	27 (8%)
"The prevalence of Autism has increased over the years"	
True	208 (63%)
False	28 (8%)
Not Sure	96 (29%)
"Autism can arise from vaccinations"	
True	7 (2%)
False	284 (86%)
Not Sure	41 (12%)
"Individuals with Autism always prefer to be alone"	
True	19 (6%)
False	286 (86%)
Not Sure	27 (8%)
"People with Autism are eccentric geniuses"	
True	33 (10%)
False	244 (73%)
Not Sure	55 (17%)
"Individuals with Autism can grow out of it"	
True	27 (8%)
False	232 (70%)
Not Sure	73 (22%)
"People with Autism require substantial medical assistance"	
True	60 (18%)
False	172 (52%)
Not Sure	100 (30%)
Knowledge Score	
Not Knowledgeable (0-4)	48 (14%)
Satisfactory (5-6)	129 (39%)
Knowledgeable (7-8)	155 (48%)

Table 4. Perceived and actual knowledge - by subgroups

Question Item	**Under 20** **n = 177**	**Over 20** **n = 155**	**p-value**
"I believe I am knowledgeable about Autism"			0.0002
Agree	72 (41%)	91 (59%)	
Disagree	27 (15%)	6 (4%)	
Neutral	78 (44%)	58 (37%)	
"Autism is a life-long developmental condition"			0.1244
True	153 (86%)	137 (88%)	
False	3 (2%)	7 (5%)	
Not Sure	21 (12%)	11 (7%)	
"Autism can be caused by poor parenting or parental behavior"			0.0831
True	2 (1%)	2 (1%)	
False	167 (94%)	136 (88%)	
Not Sure	8 (5%)	17 (11%)	
"The prevalence of Autism has increased over the years"			0.1194
True	102 (58%)	106 (68%)	
False	16 (9%)	12 (8%)	
Not Sure	59 (33%)	37 (24%)	
"Autism can arise from vaccinations"			0.0012
True	6 (3%)	1 (1%)	
False	145 (82%)	139 (90%)	
Not Sure	26 (15%)	15 (10%)	
"Individuals with Autism always prefer to be alone"			0.1348
True	7 (4%)	12 (8%)	
False	152 (86%)	134 (86%)	
Not Sure	18 (10%)	9 (6%)	
"People with Autism are eccentric geniuses"			0.0015
True	19 (11%)	14 (9%)	
False	117 (66%)	127 (82%)	
Not Sure	41 (23%)	14 (9%)	
"Individuals with Autism can grow out of it"			0.5195
True	17 (10%)	10 (6%)	
False	120 (68%)	112 (72%)	
Not Sure	40 (23%)	33 (21%)	

Table 4. (Continued)

Question Item	**Under 20 n = 177**	**Over 20 n = 155**	**p-value**
"People with Autism require substantial medical assistance"			0.8265
True	30 (17%)	30 (19%)	
False	92 (52%)	80 (52%)	
Not Sure	55 (31%)	45 (29%)	
Knowledge Score			0.1529
Not Knowledgeable (0-4)	29 (16%)	19 (12%)	
Satisfactory (5-6)	74 (42%)	55 (35%)	
Knowledgeable (7-8)	74 (42%)	81 (52%)	
Question Item	**Males n = 63**	**Females n = 174**	
"I believe I am knowledgeable about Autism"			0.2506
Agree	29 (46%)	80 (46%)	
Disagree	4 (6%)	24 (14%)	
Neutral	30 (48%)	70 (40%)	
"Autism is a life-long developmental condition"			0.9771
True	55 (87%)	151 (87%)	
False	2 (3%)	5 (3%)	
Not Sure	6 (10%)	18 (10%)	
"Autism can be caused by poor parenting or parental behavior"		1 (1%)	0.7322
True	1 (1%)	158 (91%)	
False	56 (89%)	15 (9%)	
Not Sure	6 (10%)		
"The prevalence of Autism has increased over the years"			0.8486
True	42 (67%)	109 (63%)	
False	5 (8%)	15 (9%)	
Not Sure	16 (25%)	50 (29%)	
"Autism can arise from vaccinations"			0.3757
True	2 (3%)	4 (2%)	
False	55 (87%)	141 (81%)	
Not Sure	6 (10%)	29 (17%)	
"Individuals with Autism always prefer to be alone"			0.2461
True	6 (10%)	7 (4%)	
False	53 (84%)	153 (88%)	
Not Sure	4 (6%)	14 (8%)	

Question Item	**Males n = 63**	**Females n = 174**	
"People with Autism are eccentric geniuses"			0.4011
True	4 (6%)	20 (11%)	
False	45 (71%)	124 (71%)	
Not Sure	14 (22%)	30 (17%)	
"Individuals with Autism can grow out of it"			0.1400
True	3 (5%)	16 (9%)	
False	39 (62%)	120 (69%)	
Not Sure	21 (33%)	38 (22%)	
"People with Autism require substantial medical assistance"			0.3405
True	16 (25%)	30 (17%)	
False	29 (46%)	94 (54%)	
Not Sure	18 (29%)	50 (29%)	
Knowledge Score			0.9155
Not Knowledgeable (0-4)	10 (16%)	24 (14%)	
Satisfactory (5-6)	26 (41%)	75 (43%)	
Knowledgeable (7-8)	27 (43%)	75 (43%)	
Question Item	**Family affected n = 112**	**Family unaffected n = 220**	
"I believe I am knowledgeable about Autism"			<0.0001
Agree	82 (73%)	81 (37%)	
Disagree	4 (4%)	29 (13%)	
Neutral	26 (23%)	110 (50%)	
"Autism is a life-long developmental condition"			0.1581
True	103 (92%)	187 (85%)	
False	3 (3%)	7 (3%)	
Not Sure	6 (5%)	26 (12%)	
"Autism can be caused by poor parenting or parental behavior"			0.0394
True	0 (0%)	4 (2%)	
False	97 (87%)	204 (93%)	
Not Sure	15 (13%)	12 (5%)	
"The prevalence of Autism has increased over the years"			0.1692
True	78 (70%)	130 (59%)	
False	8 (7%)	20 (9%)	
Not Sure	26 (23%)	70 (32%)	

Table 4. (Continued)

Question Item	Family affected n = 112	Family unaffected n = 220	
"Autism can arise from vaccinations"			0.5128
True	1 (1%)	6 (3%)	
False	98 (88%)	186 (85%)	
Not Sure	13 (12%)	28 (13%)	
"Individuals with Autism always prefer to be alone"			0.0983
True	10 (9%)	9 (4%)	
False	96 (86%)	190 (86%)	
Not Sure	6 (5%)	21 (10%)	
"People with Autism are eccentric geniuses"			0.3412
True	14 (13%)	19 (9%)	
False	83 (74%)	161 (73%)	
Not Sure	15 (13%)	40 (18%)	
"Individuals with Autism can grow out of it"			0.7046
True	11 (10%)	16 (7%)	
False	76 (68%)	156 (71%)	
Not Sure	25 (22%)	48 (22%)	
"People with Autism require substantial medical assistance"			0.0121
True	28 (25%)	32 (15%)	
False	60 (54%)	112 (51%)	
Not Sure	24 (21%)	76 (35%)	
Knowledge Score			0.0949
Not Knowledgeable (0-4)	16 (14%)	32 (15%)	
Satisfactory (5-6)	35 (31%)	94 (43%)	
Knowledgeable (7-8)	61 (54%)	94 (43%)	
"I believe I am knowledgeable about Autism"			0.0028
Agree	100 (58%)	63 (40%)	
Disagree	12 (7%)	21 (13%)	
Neutral	61 (35%)	75 (47%)	
"Autism is a life-long developmental condition"			0.4291
True	155 (90%)	135 (85%)	
False	4 (2%)	6 (4%)	
Not Sure	14 (8%)	18 (11%)	

Question Item	**Family affected n = 112**	**Family unaffected n = 220**	
"Autism can be caused by poor parenting or parental behavior"			0.2869
True	2 (1%)	2 (1%)	
False	153 (88%)	148 (93%)	
Not Sure	18 (10%)	9 (6%)	
"The prevalence of Autism has increased over the years"			0.5682
True	109 (63%)	99 (62%)	
False	12 (7%)	16 (10%)	
Not Sure	52 (30%)	44 (28%)	
"Autism can arise from vaccinations"			0.0482
True	4 (2%)	3 (2%)	
False	155 (90%)	129 (81%)	
Not Sure	14 (8%)	27 (17%)	
"Individuals with Autism always prefer to be alone"			0.1267
True	15 (9%)	6 (4%)	
False	146 (84%)	137 (86%)	
Not Sure	12 (7%)	16 (10%)	
"People with Autism are eccentric geniuses"			0.6948
True	15 (9%)	18 (11%)	
False	128 (74%)	116 (73%)	
Not Sure	30 (17%)	25 (16%)	
"Individuals with Autism can grow out of it"			0.0385
True	16 (9%)	11 (7%)	
False	128 (74%)	103 (65%)	
Not Sure	29 (17%)	45 (28%)	
"People with Autism require substantial medical assistance"			0.0851
True	35 (20%)	25 (16%)	
False	95 (55%)	77 (48%)	
Not Sure	43 (25%)	57 (36%)	
Knowledge Score			0.0118
Not Knowledgeable (0-4)	28 (16%)	20 (13%)	
Satisfactory (5-6)	54 (31%)	75 (47%)	
Knowledgeable (7-8)	91 (53%)	64 (40%)	

The results also indicate that 48% believed they were knowledgeable, which is an intermediate proportion to those who knew of a family member (34%) and those who knew of a friend (52%) affected by ASD. This suggests that the future prevalence may be approximately similar to today's prevalence, as the awareness is not in extreme excess of the prevalence. Future studies should follow these young adults and determine whether future prevalence will actually be similar, in a longitudinal setting.

Subgroup analyses indicates that exposure to a friend who is affected by ASD may be related to greater awareness, both perceived and actual. However, it is important to note that these survey studies are only correlational, and hence longitudinal studies should further investigate whether the exposure to a friend is predictive of the awareness level.

In conclusion, 48% believed they were knowledgeable about ASD. A greater proportion had a friend who knew of a friend affected by ASD (52%) and a smaller proportion knew of a family member affected by ASD (34%). The subgroup analyses indicate that exposure to a friend may be related to greater awareness, revealing that knowing of an individual afflicted by ASD may increase awareness. Future studies should follow young adults to chart whether the future prevalence remains the same, as suggested by our results.

ACKNOWLEDGMENTS

We would like to thank Michael Borean, Drew Hollenberg, Tharani Anpalagan, and Victoria Trasente for their support.

REFERENCES

[1] American Psychiatric Association. Diagnostic and statistical manual of mental disorders (DSM-5). Arlington, VA: American Psychiatric Association, 2013.

[2] Bailey A, Le Couteur A, Gottesman I, Bolton P, Simonoff E, Yuzda E, et al. Autism as a strongly genetic disorder: evidence from a British twin study. Psychol Med 1995;25:63-77.

[3] Marco EJ, Shuse DH. Autism-lessons from the X-chromosome. Soc Cogn Affect Neurosci 2006;1:183-93.

[4] Kothur K, Ray M, Malhi P. Correlation of autism with temporal tubers in tuberous sclerosis complex. Neurol India 2008;56:74-6.

[5] Muhle R, Trentacoste SV, Rapin I. The genetics of autism. Pediatrics 2004;113:e472-86.

[6] Bolton PF, Park RJ, Higgins JN, Griffiths PD, Pickles A. Neuro-epileptic determinants of autism spectrum disorder in tuberous sclerosis complex. Brain 2002;125:1247-55.

[7] Trottier G, Srivastava L, Walker CD. Etiology of infantile autism: A review of recent advances in genetic and neurobiological research. J Psychiatr Neurosci 1999;24:103-15.

[8] Chakrabarti S, Fombonne E. Pervasive developmental disorders in preschool children. JAMA 2001;285:3093-9.

[9] Chakrabarti S, Fombonne E. Pervasive development disorders in preschool children: confirmation of high prevalence. Am J Psychiatry 2005;162:1133-41.

[10] Bertrand J, Mars A, Boyle C, Bove F, Yeargin-Allsop M, DeCoufle P. Prevalence of autism in a United States population: The Brick Township, New Jersey, investigation. Pediatrics 2001;108:1155-61.

[11] Yeargin-Allsop M, Rice C, Karapurkar T, Doernberg N, Boyle C, Murphy C. Prevalence of autism in a US metropolitan area. JAMA 2003;289:49-55.

[12] Fombonne E, Zakarian R, Bennett A, Meng L, McLean-Heywood D. Pervasive developmental disorders in Montreal, Quebec, Canada: Prevalence and links with immunization. Pediatrics 2006;118:e139-50.

[13] Shattuck PT. The combination of diagnostic substitution to the growing administrative prevalence of autism in US special education data. Pediatrics 2006;117:1028-37.

[14] Chow R, Viehweger J, Merrick J. Are young adults aware of autism spectrum disorder? Int J Public Health 2019;11(1), in press.

[15] Chow R, Viehweger J, Anpalagan T, Yang H, Banerjee R. Awareness of autism spectrum disorder among young adults in London, Canada. Int Public Health J 2019;11(1), in press.

[16] Chow R, Viehweger J, Hollenberg D, Ho C, Ng W, Wong M. Awareness of autism spectrum disorder among young adults in Toronto, Canada. Int Public Health J 2019;11(1), in press.

[17] Chow R, Viehweger J, Murai A. Awareness of autism spectrum disorder among young adults in California, USA. Int Public Health J 2019;11(1), in press.

[18] Viehweger J, Chow R, Borean M. Awareness of autism spectrum disorder among young adults in Montreal, Canada. Int Public Health J 2019;11(1), in press.

[19] Chow R, Viehweger J. Awareness of autism spectrum disorder among young adults in Calgary, Canada. Int Public Health J 2019;11(1), in press.
[20] Viehweger J, Chow R, Goh S. Awareness of autism spectrum disorder among young adults in United Kingdom. Int Public Health J 2019;11(1), in press.
[21] Viehweger J, Chow R, Ganguli N. Awareness of autism spectrum disorder among young adults in New York State, USA. Int Public Health J 2019;11(1), in press.
[22] Viehweger J, Chow R. Awareness of autism spectrum disorder among young adults in Asia. Int Public Health J 2019;11(1), in press.
[23] Viehweger J, Chow R, Liu J. Awareness of autism spectrum disorder among young adults in Waterloo, Canada. Int Public Health J 2019;11(1), in press.
[24] Hollenberg D, Viehweger J, Chow R. Awareness of autism spectrum disorder among young adults in Hamilton, Canada. Int Public Health J 2019;11(1), in press.

SECTION FOUR: ACKNOWLEDGMENTS

In: Autism Spectrum Disorder ISBN: 978-1-53612-730-0
Editors: R. Chow, J. Viehweger et al. ©2017 Nova Science Publishers, Inc.

Chapter 14

ABOUT THE EDITORS

Ronald Chow, BMSc(C), is the Founder and Chair of the Infinitas Research Group, headquartered in London, Ontario, Canada. At the young age of 19 years old, he already has over 160 peer-reviewed publications to his name. He was the recipient of the Ontario Lieutenant Governor's Community Volunteer Award for volunteerism in his community, the Chancellor's Scholarship from Queen's University for excellent academic ability and leadership skills, the George Eastman Young Leaders Award from the University of Rochester for astounding leadership and extensive extracurricular activities, and both the Future of Western Award and Innovation Award from the University of Western Ontario as the most accomplished first-year university student leader in the areas of academics, student government, athletics and philanthropy. Email: rchow48@uwo.ca.

Jaclyn Viehweger, BMSc(C), is the Deputy Chair of Infinitas Research Group. Jaclyn is also a Varsity Cheerleader with the University of Western Ontario Mustangs. She holds the Gold Duke of Edinburgh Award for her service in the community and commitment to extracurriculars and athletics. Jaclyn graduated from Holy Name of Mary College School in Mississauga having received the Sister Celestine Giertych Social Justice Award and is now at Western University pursuing a Bachelor of Medical Sciences. Email: jviehweg@uwo.ca.

Joav Merrick, MD, MMedSci, DMSc, born and educated in Denmark is professor of pediatrics, child health and human development, Division of Pediatrics, Hadassah Hebrew University Medical Center, Mt Scopus Campus, Jerusalem, Israel and Kentucky Children's Hospital, University of Kentucky, Lexington, Kentucky United States and professor of public health at the Center for Healthy Development, School of Public Health, Georgia State University, Atlanta, United States, the medical director of the Health Services, Division for Intellectual and Developmental Disabilities, Ministry of Social Affairs and Social Services, Jerusalem, the founder and director of the National Institute of Child Health and Human Development in Israel. Numerous publications in the field of pediatrics, child health and human development, rehabilitation, intellectual disability, disability, health, welfare, abuse, advocacy, quality of life and prevention. Received the Peter Sabroe Child Award for outstanding work on behalf of Danish Children in 1985 and the International LEGO-Prize ("The Children's Nobel Prize") for an extraordinary contribution towards improvement in child welfare and well-being in 1987. Email: jmerrick@zahav.net.il.

In: Autism Spectrum Disorder ISBN: 978-1-53612-730-0
Editors: R. Chow, J. Viehweger et al. ©2017 Nova Science Publishers, Inc.

Chapter 15

About Infinitas Research Group, London, Ontario, Canada

Infinitas Research Group (IRG) was founded in 2017, and is currently headquartered in London, Ontario, Canada. Research associates are based around the globe (across Canada, United States, Europe, Asia and Australia), allowing for IRG to conduct research studies on an international scale.

IRG has a special interest in public health issues, and specializes into studying the adolescent and young adult population. IRG has collaborated with many other organizations and has published over 40 papers in its first six months related to topics such as bicycle safety and Alzheimer's disease.

Contact

Ronald Chow
Founder and Chair,
Infinitas Research Group,
London, Ontario, Canada
Email: rchow48@uwo.ca

In: Autism Spectrum Disorder ISBN: 978-1-53612-730-0
Editors: R. Chow, J. Viehweger et al. ©2017 Nova Science Publishers, Inc.

Chapter 16

About the National Institute of Child Health and Human Development in Israel

The National Institute of Child Health and Human Development (NICHD) in Israel was established in 1998 as a virtual institute under the auspices of the Medical Director, Ministry of Social Affairs and Social Services in order to function as the research arm for the Office of the Medical Director. In 1998 the National Council for Child Health and Pediatrics, Ministry of Health and in 1999 the Director General and Deputy Director General of the Ministry of Health endorsed the establishment of the NICHD.

Mission

The mission of a National Institute for Child Health and Human Development in Israel is to provide an academic focal point for the scholarly interdisciplinary study of child life, health, public health, welfare, disability, rehabilitation, intellectual disability and related aspects of human development. This mission includes research, teaching, clinical work, information and public service activities in the field of child health and human development.

Service and academic activities

Over the years many activities became focused in the south of Israel due to collaboration with various professionals at the Faculty of Health Sciences (FOHS) at the Ben Gurion University of the Negev (BGU). Since 2000 an affiliation with the Zusman Child Development Center at the Pediatric Division of Soroka University Medical Center has resulted in collaboration around the establishment of the Down Syndrome Clinic at that center. In 2002 a full course on "Disability" was established at the Recanati School for Allied Professions in the Community, FOHS, BGU and in 2005 collaboration was started with the Primary Care Unit of the faculty and disability became part of the master of public health course on "Children and society". In the academic year 2005-2006 a one semester course on "Aging with disability" was started as part of the master of science program in gerontology in our collaboration with the Center for Multidisciplinary Research in Aging. In 2010 collaborations with the Division of Pediatrics, Hadassah Hebrew University Medical Center, Jerusalem, Israel around the National Down Syndrome Center and teaching students and residents about intellectual and developmental disabilities as part of their training at this campus.

Research activities

The affiliated staff have over the years published work from projects and research activities in this national and international collaboration. In the year 2000 the International Journal of Adolescent Medicine and Health and in 2005 the International Journal on Disability and Human Development of De Gruyter Publishing House (Berlin and New York) were affiliated with the National Institute of Child Health and Human Development. From

2008 also the International Journal of Child Health and Human Development (Nova Science, New York), the International Journal of Child and Adolescent Health (Nova Science) and the Journal of Pain Management (Nova Science) affiliated and from 2009 the International Public Health Journal (Nova Science) and Journal of Alternative Medicine Research (Nova Science). All peer-reviewed international journals.

National collaborations

Nationally the NICHD works in collaboration with the Faculty of Health Sciences, Ben Gurion University of the Negev; Department of Physical Therapy, Sackler School of Medicine, Tel Aviv University; Autism Center, Assaf HaRofeh Medical Center; National Rett and PKU Centers at Chaim Sheba Medical Center, Tel HaShomer; Department of Physiotherapy, Haifa University; Department of Education, Bar Ilan University, Ramat Gan, Faculty of Social Sciences and Health Sciences; College of Judea and Samaria in Ariel and in 2011 affiliation with Center for Pediatric Chronic Diseases and National Center for Down Syndrome, Department of Pediatrics, Hadassah Hebrew University Medical Center, Mount Scopus Campus, Jerusalem.

International collaborations

Internationally with the Department of Disability and Human Development, College of Applied Health Sciences, University of Illinois at Chicago; Strong Center for Developmental Disabilities, Golisano Children's Hospital at Strong, University of Rochester School of Medicine and Dentistry, New York; Centre on Intellectual Disabilities, University of Albany, New York; Centre for Chronic Disease Prevention and Control, Health Canada, Ottawa; Chandler Medical Center and Children's Hospital, Kentucky Children's Hospital, Section of Adolescent Medicine, University of Kentucky, Lexington; Chronic Disease Prevention and Control Research

Center, Baylor College of Medicine, Houston, Texas; Division of Neuroscience, Department of Psychiatry, Columbia University, New York; Institute for the Study of Disadvantage and Disability, Atlanta; Center for Autism and Related Disorders, Department Psychiatry, Children's Hospital Boston, Boston; Department of Pediatric and Adolescent Medicine, Western Michigan University Homer Stryker MD School of Medicine, Kalamazoo, Michigan, United States; Department of Paediatrics, Child Health and Adolescent Medicine, Children's Hospital at Westmead, Westmead, Australia; International Centre for the Study of Occupational and Mental Health, Düsseldorf, Germany; Centre for Advanced Studies in Nursing, Department of General Practice and Primary Care, University of Aberdeen, Aberdeen, United Kingdom; Quality of Life Research Center, Copenhagen, Denmark; Nordic School of Public Health, Gottenburg, Sweden, Scandinavian Institute of Quality of Working Life, Oslo, Norway; The Department of Applied Social Sciences (APSS) of The Hong Kong Polytechnic University Hong Kong.

Targets

Our focus is on research, international collaborations, clinical work, teaching and policy in health, disability and human development and to establish the NICHD as a permanent institute in Israel in order to conduct model research and together with the four university schools of public health/medicine in Israel establish a national master and doctoral program in disability and human development at the institute to secure the next generation of professionals working in this often non-prestigious/low-status field of work.

Contact

Joav Merrick, MD, MMedSci, DMSc
Professor of Pediatrics
Medical Director, Health Services, Division for Intellectual and Developmental Disabilities, Ministry of Social Affairs and Social Services, PO Box 1260, IL-91012 Jerusalem, Israel.
E-mail: jmerrick@zahav.net.il

In: Autism Spectrum Disorder ISBN: 978-1-53612-730-0
Editors: R. Chow, J. Viehweger et al. ©2017 Nova Science Publishers, Inc.

Chapter 17

ABOUT THE BOOK SERIES "DISABILITY STUDIES"

Disability studies is a book series with publications from a multidisciplinary group of researchers, practitioners and clinicians for an international professional forum interested in the broad spectrum of disability, intellectual disability, health and human development.

- Reiter S. Disability from a humanistic perspective: Towards a better quality of life. New York: Nova Science, 2008
- Knotkova H, Cruciani R, Merrick J, eds. Pain. Brain stimulation in the treatment of pain. New York: Nova Science, 2010.
- Prasher VP, ed. Contemporary issues in intellectual disabilities. New York: Nova Science, 2010.
- Lotan M, Merrick J, eds. Rett syndrome: Therapeutic interventions. New York: Nova Science, 2011.
- Satgé D, Merrick J, eds. Cancer in children and adults with intellectual disabilities: Current research aspects. New York: Nova Science, 2011.
- Knotkova H, Cruciani RA, Merrick J, eds. Neural plasticity in chronic pain. New York: Nova Science, 2011.
- Prasher VP. Down syndrome and dementia. A comprehensive and historical review. New York: Nova Science, 2012.

- Merrick J, Aspler S, Morad M, eds. Disability and chronic disease. New York: Nova Science, 2013.
- Tse MMY, Merrick J. Pain and the elderly. New York: Nova Science, 2013.
- Brown RI, Faragher RM, eds. Quality of life and intellectual disability: Knowledge application to other social and educational challenges. New York: Nova Science, 2014.
- Grenon I. From one century to the next: A history of Wrentham State School and the Institutional Model in Massachusetts. New York: Nova Science, 2014.
- Sharkey PM, Merrick J, eds. Virtual reality: People with special needs. New York: Nova Science, 2014.
- Sharkey PM, Merrick J, eds. Virtual reality: Rehabilitation in motor, cognitive and sensorial disorders. New York: Nova Science, 2014.
- Merrick J, Greydanus DE, Patel DR, eds. Intellectual disability: Some current issues New York: Nova Science, 2014.
- Pareto L, Sharkey PM, Merrick J, eds. Technology, rehabilitation and empowerment of people with special needs. New York: Nova Science, 2015.
- Sharkey PM, Merrick J, eds. Recent advances on using virtual reality technologies for rehabilitation. New York: Nova Science, 2016.
- Omar HA, Patel DR, Greydanus DE, Merrick J, eds. Pediatric pain: Current aspects. New York: Nova Science, 2016.
- Palusci VJ, Nazer D, Greydanus DE, Merrick J, eds. Child abuse: Children with disabilities. New York: Nova Science, 2017.
- Powell W, Rizzo A, Sharkey PM, Merrick J, eds. Virtual reality: Recent advances in virtual rehabilitation system design. New York: Nova Science, 2017.
- Powell W, Rizzo A, Sharkey PM, Merrick J, eds. Rehabilitation: Innovations and challenges in the use of virtual reality technologies. New York: Nova Science, 2017.
- Powell W, Sharkey PM, Rizzo A, Merrick J, eds. Virtual reality: Recent advances for health and wellbeing. New York: Nova Science, 2017.

Contact

Professor Joav Merrick, MD, MMedSci, DMSc
Medical Director, Health Services, Division for Intellectual and Developmental Disabilities, Ministry of Social Affairs and Social Services, PO Box 1260
IL-91012 Jerusalem, Israel
E-mail: jmerrick@internet-zahav.net

SECTION FIVE: INDEX

INDEX

N

P

Q

R

S

T

U

V

W

Y